Gifted Inspirations

An Inspirational Treasury of Writings To Transform Your Thinking About Your Gift

Barbara Bryant

WestBow
PRESS

WestBow Press books may be ordered through booksellers or by contacting:

WestBow Press
A Division of Thomas Nelson
1663 Liberty Drive
Bloomington, IN 47403
www.westbowpress.com
1-(866) 928-1240

Because of the dynamic nature of the Internet, any Web addresses or links contained in this book may have changed since publication and may no longer be valid. The views expressed in this work are solely those of the author and do not necessarily reflect the views of the publisher, and the publisher hereby disclaims any responsibility for them.

ISBN: 978-1-4497-0329-5 (sc)
ISBN: 978-1-4497-0331-8 (hc)
ISBN: 978-1-4497-0330-1 (e)

Library of Congress Control Number: 2010931017

Unless otherwise noted, all Scriptures taken from the King James Version of the Bible.

Definitions are taken from Merriam-Webster's Collegiate Dictionary, Eleventh Edition copyright © 2008 by Merriam-Webster, Incorporated

Printed in the United States of America

WestBow Press rev. date: 6/28/2010

In honor of my two sons
Steven and Stedmon
with prayers that they will explore the vast riches and
depths of God's power, wisdom and grace and
use their gifts to love and serve Him.

Dedication

This book is dedicated to Jessie Mae Stewart, my incredibly gifted mom. Everyone should have a mother as loving, supportive, and fun to be around as you. There are so many wonderful stories I could tell the world about your persona. But I think this one will sum up your love and care for me. In 1993, I lost my little talking doll Drowsy that you purchased for me when I was age five. I was distraught because Drowsy had become a part of my life over the years.

After telling you how much I missed Drowsy a few months before my birthday, unbeknownst to me you began searching every store in the area until you found this 1960 production. You then called me on my 44th birthday and informed me that you had the best birthday gift in the world. At the time, I could not think of what that gift could be. In the meantime, you cleaned Drowsy's white polka-dot pajamas and combed her hair into place and made her look brand new again. You then placed Drowsy inside a white pillow case.

When I arrived to your home that evening, you told me that my birthday gift was inside the pillow case placed next to you on the sofa. For a moment, I said, "Is my mom suffering from Alzheimer's?" Very hesitantly, I reached in the pillow case and pulled out the most precious birthday gift ever. It was Drowsy. What a wonderful birthday surprise! I began to cry. This unforgettable moment was just another example of how much you love me. You sacrificed so much for me, and did it willingly. For that, I love you from the depths of my heart.

It is my joy to dedicate this book to you. You have been my biggest supporter and have stuck by me through thick and thin. Most importantly, you taught me how to love Jesus and to be true to oneself. I love you, Mom.

Jessie (Mom), Barbara and Drowsy

Acknowledgments

I'm one of those people who plans her Oscar acceptance speech years in advance, even though I have never worked on any project that could possibly lead to winning an Academy Award. If this book were eligible for an Oscar, my speech would start with profuse thanks to the wonderful mentors in my life: Pastor James A. Lewis, Sr., Dr. Barbara McCoo Lewis, Pastor Andrew Jackson, Sr. and Mrs. Lottie Jackson. I would like to thank Pastor Jeffrey Lewis and Mrs. Floetta Lewis who have contributed greatly to the quality of my spiritual life over the past four years. This book could not have happened without the enthusiasm of Nancy Williams, my Senior Editor. Next, I would say thanks to my lifetime best friend, Carletta Adams for her simple suggestion before I even started writing, "Please give me something practical," she said. And I would thank Stephanie Young, Margarette Lawson-Walker and Honey Butler for always knowing the right time to encourage me during this season of my life. I would acknowledge my two wonderful sons, Steven and Stedmon, who would be in the audience smiling. Without question my two sons have both felt the pain and joy of this project. I would then blow a kiss to them both. After the kiss, I would throw out the names of my siblings: Evelyn, Mahalia, Marie, Victor, Cynthia, Stanley and Yolanda to whom I owe either thanks or money. A thank you would be in order to Mr. E.K. Tillman for always extending his wisdom and support in difficult times. I would also plead for all of us to live in harmony and peace and to exercise the gift God has so freely given to us. And finally, to my Creator, my God--I would thank Him for providing me the right words when I was at a loss for them. I am only the author of this book; He is the author of my life.

With heartfelt appreciation,

Barbara

A **gift** or a present is the transfer of something without the expectation of receiving something in return. Although gift-giving might involve an expectation of reciprocity, a gift is meant to be free.

Contents

Introduction: You Are Gifted To Be a Gift

You Are Gifted To Be a Gift

Your skills and abilities, your unique personhood are God's precious gifts to you. Gifts are also God's call to you. You acknowledge acceptance by putting them into service.

Gifts: Everyone has one or more gifts or abilities they display either knowingly or unknowingly. In spite of who you are, good or bad, black or white, we all have gifts, talents, attributes and acquired skills.

God gives us specific gifts and uses them as the primary avenue with which to bless others. Any gift that's left unopened or is disregarded is useless.

The miracle comes when, rather than hoarding it, we share it with others, so that they may see and feel evidence of God's amazing love. How little it takes to demonstrate the presence and power of God through our gifts.

What Would Happen If...

Stop right now--and imagine for just a moment, that you are watching a movie and it is entitled *All That God Might Have Done With My Life If I had Totally Surrender To Him.*

- Imagine seeing what He might have done with your financial resources--if you had trusted Him and been generous.

- Imagine what He might have done in your relationships--if you had trusted Him enough to be fully loving and caring.

- Imagine what He might have done with your ministry--if you had pursued spiritual growth and consistently kept your hunger and thirst for righteousness.

- Imagine the doors He would have opened in ministry --if you had only stayed in the will of God.

- Imagine the anointing on your life--if you had fasted and prayed like you should.

- Imagine what He might have done with your gifts--if you had used them to glorify Him.

In this movie, you see the person you could have become but did not. You see lives you could have touched, but did not, because you never followed your calling. You didn't allow your abilities to be cultivated and deployed, because you never totally surrendered to God. You never fully opened up the gift God gave you--to win souls for Christ.

Now, I know that this movie will never exist or hit the billboard charts. But just imagine that now the movie is over. What is your response? Having seen what might have been, are you ready to line up with the will of God for your life? Are you ready to minimize the gap between what will be and what might have been?

Think about it for just a moment. What has the Lord given to you that you need to invest in the kingdom of God? Yes, He's given you power. Yes, he's give you strength, but He has also given you A GIFT.

Each of God's children has been given a gift, chosen by the Master, because none of us gets to choose our gifts. In the same way we can't choose our genetic makeup, our families or our genders, we can't choose our gifts.

Everybody receives a gift. And it is important that we recognize what God has gifted us with--and what He intends for us to do with that gift.

The Lord of the gift has entrusted His property to us. And along with that gift we have been given a choice whether or not we will open and use what was given.

You see, any time a gift is given, the recipient must respond in one of two ways. In the first case scenario, the recipient believes that the gift is so valuable it seems too risky even to remove it from the box. Meaning that when I open it and pull it from the box, things may not always go well because the gift may at times be inadequately used. It may not always be admired and appreciated by others. It may get broken, shattered, or even get overlooked at times. So we say, "I'm going to keep it in the box, because taking it out of the box is always a risk."

The second way says the gift is so valuable that the recipient says: "No matter what happens I dare not leave it in the box." If the gift is not taken out of the box, it will never be used at all. To leave the gift unopened is the worst tragedy of all, because it frustrates and disregards the desire of the giver. The gift cannot accomplish its intended purpose if it stays inside its package.

The practical implication is I must open up and come to appreciate what the Lord of the Gift has given me and seize every opportunity to use it.

Too often Christians use the excuse that because of circumstances we cannot exercise our gift to help someone. We play the "when-then" game.

- When I feel confident, then I'll try to use my gift.
- When I get over my problem, then I'll help someone else.
- When I can first help myself then I can help someone else.
- When I become financially stable, then I'll give.

We waste immeasurable time and effort waiting for a *"when"* that never comes.

The fact is we have each been given a gift. The question is what have you done with what God gave you? Who have you helped? Who have you supported? Who have you nurtured? Who have you cared for? Who have you lent a hand to? Who have you assisted? Who have you looked after? Who have you encouraged?

What God wants to know is what have you done with your gift? You don't have to answer, but consider the parable of the talents:

Matthew 25:14 says: "For it is just like a man about to go on a journey, who called his own slaves and entrusted his own possessions to them. And to one he gave five talents; to another, two, and to another, one, each according to his own ability; and he went on his journey."

In this parable there are several things that stand out. First, there are varying amounts of gifts. One man gets five, another two, and a third gets one talent. In this regard, I think Jesus is simply explaining life as we experience it.

Some people are gifted in ways that are visible and obvious to others. Others are gifted in ways that remain quiet and unseen. The variable that matters is what each servant does with what he's been given.

Jesus makes it perfectly clear in the parable that the size of the gift is not what's important. Even though the first servant receives a gift much larger than the second, Jesus responds in identical fashion to both the first and the second servant.

It's crucial to understand the issue is not the visible level of giftedness and calling. The size and visibility are not what counts in the long run. That's why as Christians we shouldn't compare our gifts to those of other people. This is because comparison will either result in pride or misery, depending on how successful we think we are. Our task is to identify, cultivate and invest our gifts, no matter how large or small, to bring glory to God.

The Lord of the Gift is very wise. He knew exactly what He was doing when He created you. He is well pleased that you exist. He has entrusted to you everything you need to fulfill the purpose for which you were created. And at the end of the day–God is not going to ask, "Why you didn't lead someone else's life? He's not going to ask, "Why you didn't invest someone else's gift?" His question is not going to be "What did you do with what you didn't have? Instead He's going to ask–"What did you do with what I gave you?"

When God asked the third servant why he hid his talent, he replied, "For I knew that you were a hard man reaping where you do not sow, and I was afraid, so I hid what you gave me" (Mathew 25:24). One of the most fundamental aspects of this story is that the servant is judged, not for doing bad things, but for doing *nothing*. He didn't steal or embezzle or defraud. He merely buried his gift. And Jesus uses two serious words to describe him: wicked and lazy. He was slothful.

Now, I know we don't use these two words very often. Nowadays hardly anyone would admit to laziness. When someone is asked in a job interview about personal weaknesses, what is their answer? "I push myself too hard. My standards are too high. I expect too much of myself." When was the last time you heard someone admit: my problem is that I'm just too darn lazy"? Regrettably, so many Christians suffer from the same basic problem.

When it comes to identifying the lazy, the finger of blame points mostly to Christians. The unsaved can't be held accountable for something they never pledged to uphold. Believers are the ones responsible for using their gift to carry the banner of the Great Commission.

Laziness, as it relates to believers, is the tendency to do nothing in the face of opportunity. Laziness is also the failure of a person to properly manage the time and resources God has provided. Because we all have different gifts and abilities, the quantity and quality of our work can never be a true indicator of dedication. One person may be highly skilled at a task, yet lack the motivation to be productive. Someone else may have limited skills, yet choose to overcome shortcomings by putting forth more effort.

Because no action is required in the sin of laziness, it is one of the easiest of the seven deadly sins to commit. Unlike with pride, envy, anger, greed, gluttony and lust, slothfulness is performed through a passive response.

Jesus came down so hard on the third servant simply because of *inactivity*. He was idle and immobile. He did not open his gift to help anyone else. He was emphatically lazy.

Have you ever thought "What does God do all day? The biblical writers tell us what God does in a single phrase: He works!

In Genesis 2:2, it says "And on the seventh day God ended his work and he rested." It does not say that God went into retirement. Even the psalmist is quite clear that the universe does not run on its own; it is run by God. Psalms 104 (and I'm summarizing here), says, He watereth the hills from his chambers. He causeth the grass to grow for the cattle. Thou makest darkness, and it is night. O LORD, how manifold are thy works!

The Psalmist also said that God will "neither sleep nor slumber" but is always guiding and protecting His flock (Psalms 121:4). In other words, the God of the Bible is predominantly a worker. He is highly interested in, understands the joy of--and is deeply committed to work. And because we were made in God's image--we were created to work. We were made to create, to lead, study, heal, cultivate, teach, help and care for others.

In this story, the Parable of the Talents--it further emphasizes the need for personal preparation and faithful service to God. It points out that not all are expected to produce the same results but all are to be faithful with what they are given.

The first two servants doubled their money. Each of them produced results and was commended by God: "Well done...good and faithful servant" and is promised a kingdom to rule (Mathew 25:21). But the last servant hid his one talent in the earth. He failed to understand the real generosity of God who wanted to use him and allow him to experience the joy of ministry, evangelism and outreach.

The fact that the third servant is called "wicked, slothful and unprofitable" (Mathew 25:26) indicates that he was *not a true disciple of God*. And I believe the point God wanted to make from this example is this: true believers produce results in the kingdom of God. Those who refuse the talent of soul-winning and personal evangelism reveal that they do not really love people. And therefore, their salvation is in question.

Your spiritual gift is God-given. What God has put in you, He intends for you to use. Seize the opportunity. Don't be sidetracked or distracted by others who have failed to open their gift. Have you noticed that there is a world in desperate need out there, and a great God calling you to be a part of something bigger than yourself?

- Lives need to be touched
- Needs to be met
- Sick bodies waiting to be healed
- Sin-sick souls longing for salvation
- Broken and wounded hearts in dire need of God's love

And the Lord has given us a supply of gifts, talents, power, knowledge, strength, and resources not to be popular, not to be well-liked, not to be accepted, not to be admired, not to be grand. The Lord of the gift has given you and I these abilities for ministry, the crucial part of our calling.

We were given gifts to serve God and His creation. That's why God gave us the greatest gift - the gift of Himself. And He gave it to us so we could give it to others. The Word of God says, "As each one has received a gift, minister it to one another, as good stewards of the manifold grace of God" (1 Peter 4:10).

You are gifted for a reason. You have not been made exceptional, highly anointed, and powerful to walk in arrogance and self-importance. Ministry doors are not opening for you just so you can boast about how often you speak or draw attention to yourself. God brings your gift before men so they can recognize, not you, but the God within you.

The reason you are gifted to sing, teach, exhort, give and show mercy, is for the kingdom of God. The anointing you have to preach or prophecy is for the kingdom of God. All ministry gifts, whether speaking or serving are to be expressed in such a way that Jesus can bring praise to his Father, because he is worthy of glory and power.

Now is the time to open up your gift and go to work.

The writings in *Gifted Inspirations* were written to motivate, build-up, strengthen or help you discover the gift within you. It is my desire that it will offer keys to help you release your gift to the world.

Share the gift. Live out the gift. Let the gift unfold, because you have been Gifted to Be a Gift.

Part One: The Gift of Change

Spiritual principles do not change, but we do. Whether we like it or not, our lives are constantly changing. Dramatic endings and beginnings seem more prevalent than usual. Things we thought were stable and secure seem less so, and things we thought distant possibilities have come strangely close.

The truth is change is good. Every change—even the most difficult and painful, gives us the miraculous gift of personal transformation. By fixing our eyes on the one thing that does not change, Jesus Christ, we can use change as challenge to grow and become who we are capable of being.

As we change, the world changes.

THE TESTING OF TRIALS

At certain times in our lives we experience changes that turn our lives upside down, and when things seem impossibly desperate we may even find ourselves wondering what God was thinking to allow it. And yet He can take even the most difficult of circumstances and turn them around for our good. He does it all the time, if we're discerning enough to see it.

In fact, the purpose of trials is to draw us to Him. Think about this: if you had no troubles, would you need Him at all? Would you call upon Him and spend intimate time alone with Him in that secret place if you had no need for His company? Rather unlikely, is it not?

Back in the Garden of Eden, God created Adam and Eve for relationship, because He loved nothing better than spending time with them. Scripture says they walked and talked together in the cool of the day, sharing their hearts, and listening to each others' interests. Now that's true intimacy. And God feels the exact same way about us today. He wants to know what we think and how we feel. He wants to know our likes and dislikes, what bothers us, and what causes us pain or great joy. Now keep in mind that as an omniscient being He already knows all these things. But if that is so, why would He need to talk to us at all? Intimacy. He loves the closeness that relationship brings, and He (Jesus) died to make that happen.

So, to get back to the point: painful suffering as an agent of change, here is what we must know. First, Scripture says He promises never to leave or forsake us (Hebrews 13:5). He is actually in our suffering with us, weeping when we weep and rejoicing when we rejoice, closer than the dearest friend we could dare to dream up. In those times of deep grief, when we think our hearts will break, feeling we will die of the pain, we need to run to Him because He gets it. He gets how lonely we are, how lost, hopeless and isolated we feel. And He wants to wrap us in His warm embrace and rock us on His lap and press our heads against His chest and say, "I get it, baby. Go ahead and cry, because I'm here for you. And I promise it's going to be all right as long as you just hold onto Me."

There's only one hitch to this warm scenario, and that is our response to our suffering. If we shake our fists at God and cry in anger, "How could you do this to me? I hate you!" He grieves because, in the first place, He didn't make it happen. These kinds of things are merely stages of life we go through if we stay alive long enough. And why should we be exempt from suffering when others go through it every day of the week?

This brings up another point. We set ourselves up for a terrible shock if we think being believers actually exempts us from suffering. Remember the saying, "Into each life a little rain must fall"? And "The rain falls on the just and the unjust"? The only real difference between believers and unbelievers is the capacity to run to God for shelter in our times of storm.

During our storms, we must go to God and get real with Him, spilling everything that's heavy on our hearts lest it crush us under the load. We can let go of the huge weight of pain and actually dump it at His feet, because He is capable of handling what is entirely too heavy for us to deal with. In case it's not obvious, we humans weren't designed to carry heavy emotional loads for long periods of time without relief. When this happens, it can negatively affect our health. But in His presence, the wonderful secret place behind the throne of God, we can sit with Him and let His comforting Holy Spirit touch those places with that precious healing oil, the Balm of Gilead Scripture talks about. And then, in spite of the fact that our circumstances have not changed, we feel better and are encouraged that someone has identified with us right in the middle of our pain.

And don't imagine for a moment that your grief will be wasted. For when you've come through victorious, *and you will*--God will use you and your new and powerful life message to impact the lives of others who are now where you were in your pain. And they will find comfort knowing that you can, in the same way, get into their pain with them. They will be encouraged to know there will be an end to that pain, and that people do emerge whole on the other side. They will listen when you share that God is alive and well on Planet Earth, and truly cares about the tiniest details of their lives. And they will begin to think about these things, and perhaps consider the truth, that there is a God who longs to welcome them into His salvation. That's what suffering and change are all about—being tools in the Master's hands to demonstrate the incredible love of God to those who are lost and dying without Him.

In tough times of change, even those that turn our lives upside down, we can change our perspective from negative to hopeful realizing that it's just one more opportunity to let God be God. We can even go so far as to say, "I'm helpless here, Lord, with no options, so it's time for You to shine and do what You do best. Comfort and carry me right now, and let this time of change to be used to lift up the name of Jesus. Use it to minister to others, so that my light would so shine to glorify my Father who is in heaven." In that place you will find hope, peace and new joy, bubbling up like a spring whose water cannot be stopped. And in the process, you will have exercised your faith and put heaven in motion, because God thrives in this kind of situation. In fact, He's searching the world over for those who will stand in faith, no matter how dark the situation and believe He will come through for them. Does that describe you? I pray that it is so.

Scripture Reading:

1 Thessalonians 3:3
That no man should be moved by these afflictions: for yourselves know that we are appointed thereunto.

God Wants To Shift You and Lift You

Do you know what season you're in? Are you ready for the next level? Or are you leaving skid marks as God summons you to move on? Well, I have an announcement to make: It's transition time! To transition means to move on and to change, and with that change comes an opportunity for another, deeper level of growth--a time when God is telling you to take a few steps forward.

Let's face it--God is always changing us. He is always transforming us and molding us into something different, something better than we are. In the Word, God even refers to Himself as a potter and to us as His clay (Isaiah 64:8). A lump of clay is shaped into a container and then refined in fire until it is becomes a beautiful, solid, and useful vessel. Only then is it worthy of use.

We all hate change, don't we? But it's essential if we are to be useful to God. Change can be a major source of energy to drive us forward, and help us cut our own path. On the other hand, while change is never comfortable it is a fact of life as well as the will of God. The truth is, we begin the process of change when we accept Christ into our hearts and move deeper in relationship with God, in obedience, by listening and obeying His voice. We also change as we grow in age and maturity.

The key to dealing with change is to empower ourselves. While we may not be able to predict forks in the road, we can control how we deal with them. After all the Word of God says, "They shall go from strength to strength..." (Psalms 84:7).

While change can often be positive, most Christians are conditioned to resist it. Although we may be unfulfilled in certain aspects of life and ministry, we are often comfortable in the world as we know it. Yet remaining in a comfort zone can often be more dangerous than stepping out of it.

Webster's Dictionary defines change as "the passing from one condition or place to another." It is clear from this description that change comes to "shift us" or to "lift us." Are you ready for God to shift things around in your life? Are you ready for Him to lift some things out of your life? Are you ready for new and better opportunities--ready to step into new and unchartered territories? If so, change must take place. You can no longer remain the same if God is calling you to a higher level of ministry. If you stay longer in a place than God requires, both *you* and *it* will suffer.

There are two types of change: chosen change, and unchosen change. Each comes with a different set of emotions, reactions and coping mechanisms. *Chosen change* can be defined as a conscious choice a person makes to change something. This kind of change happens within one's sphere of influence gives the individual control over the choice to change. *Unchosen change*, or 'change that chooses you,' is much different. In this situation, the decision to change is not made by the individual, and the control is outside his sphere of influence. It is much more difficult to cope with, and if not properly handled can have a negative impact.

Regardless of which situation we're in, our unchanging God wants to shift us and lift us so we can transition to the next dimension in Him. Trust me; though it might seem otherwise, this change is not from the devil. God is at work in the situation. And when He changes our plans, we can rest assured that what He has prepared for us will be far better than what we have prepared for ourselves. Jeremiah 29:11 says, "For I know the plans I have for you," declares the LORD, "plans to prosper you and not to harm you, plans to give you hope and a future."

God is molding us into vessels to glorify Him. So whatever course your life is taking, be a high-speed adapter, believing that God is providentially and sovereignly changing your direction because He has a better plan in mind for your next season with Him.

Scripture Reading:

Daniel 2:21- 22
And he changeth the times and the seasons: he removeth kings, and setteth up kings: he giveth wisdom unto the wise, and knowledge to them that know understanding: He revealeth the deep and secret things: he knoweth what is in the darkness, and the light dwelleth with him.

That End Is Your Next New Beginning!

There is always a great deal of fanfare over endings. The end of tournaments, end of life, the end of businesses, the end of relationships and the end of another year. Do you ever wonder why things have to end?

Without the end of something there can be no new beginning of something else.

Most beginnings are not merely once-in-a-lifetime events. In fact, every day is a new beginning. In the same way the end of childhood ushers in adulthood, and the end of sin begins salvation. The end of sunrise brings sunset. The end of darkness is the beginning of light. The end of life begins death, while the end of physical death brings eternal life to those who know Christ as Savior.

Beginnings are often fearful, for we can't see the end or know how it will alter our lives. However, without endings we lose the ability to live to our fullest potential.

You have probably encountered many endings in your lifetime. Some may have been overwhelming, but as you look back you can see that even a traumatic end actually ushered in a brand new and positive life experience.

Beginnings require us to let go of yesterday in order to live today. They require us to let go of the old to prepare for the new. And even if you have regrets you must let go, so the wounds of the past do not hinder the future. Perhaps yesterday's end was a life-altering event, such as a loss, a missed opportunity or an error in judgment. In order to take full of advantage of new opportunities we must lay the wreckage of the past at the cross, and let it go. Instead of saying, "What if," try saying, "What's next?"

If we spend too much time pining for the past, we may miss God's blessings in the present. And we end up dreaming about what used to be instead of giving thanks for what we have right now. The devil knows this, and that's why he uses our hazy memories of yesterday to trip us up spiritually. If only he can get us yearning for what used to be, he can distract us from what God has for us in the future.

We have the power (Ephesians 3:20) to put the past behind us. By releasing the defunct, extraneous, and burdensome objects and obligations weighing you down, you create space to step into what's next and gather the energy and courage to move forward.

Every day is a new beginning. It's a gift from God. Treat it that way. Who knows what the next ending will mean for your next new beginning.

Scripture Reading:

Isaiah 42:9
Behold, the former things are come to pass, and new things do I declare: before they spring forth, I tell you of them.

Ecclesiastes 7:8
The end of a matter is better than its beginning, and patience is better than pride.

Tested For Release

I read in a magazine that a large software company had released a new beta version of its popular new product. The term "beta" means it's still being tested, although it's already been released on a limited scale. In other words, before the product can be fully released to the general public, it has to be repeatedly tested for effectiveness and functionality. Before manufacturers spend a fortune in promotion, they need to know if their product will work outside the lab. So they test the product under the most stringent test conditions, and once it passes the test, then it is fully released.

God spoke to me immediately upon reading that article. "I had to test you, before I could release you." This brought to mind some of the valuable lessons God taught me in my testing phase.

The process of releasing gifted people to greater authority requires many levels of testing, the next more stringent than the last. And as we did in school, we must pass the lower level tests before proceeding to the higher level. As with the beta testing illustration, we're only released to the public if we pass the test. Right now, I would say that most Christians are in the beta stage: they've been released to a limited group for testing. Because God desires to see how well we do outside the church setting, He sends us to small test groups that may consist of co-workers, friends, neighbors and even our families. These small test groups may be facing problems such as unexpected physical ailments, financial hardships, job losses, relationship problems, and other heartaches.

I have learned that during the time of "limited release" we go through a variety of tests before being released to the larger, general public. I have ascertained that when God tests us, He does not descend into our thought-life with a loud public announcement that warns, "This is a test. This is only a test." Instead, when God gets ready to test us, it appears without forewarning. However, the test is designed to examine *what we are* and *who we are* under stress, in real life conditions.

You see, God doesn't care how good we look on the outside. He wants to test the quality of what's inside us. He is more interested that we have right attitudes and responses than clever, pat answers. He wants to know if we can function under adverse conditions, spiritual warfare and stress.

The truth is: He will test the quality of His work in us. Remember the Lord's conversation with Satan? God asked, "Have you considered my servant Job?" (Job 1:8).

While most product testing is done under controlled laboratory conditions God tests us out in the real world, often just before the release of a double portion, which is exactly what happened to Job. Job was a righteous man of great influence in his culture when God took him through a terrible test. However, the awful price he paid for that test was more than rewarded by his blessings once the test was complete and he passed with flying colors.

When teaching about Job we often end the story by saying Job's wealth and influence increased greatly as a result of his test, but the reality is, that is not how his story ends. Rather, we need to understand that God has since used the story of Job to touch the lives of billions. The truth is that before his test, Job's range of influence reached only his immediate culture, while since that time, his integrity has inspired entire nations throughout history.

From the story of Job we can grasp the truth that our current trials are not just for our benefit.

Could it be that you are the Moses, whom God is testing, so He can use you to deliver multitudes of God's children from bondage?

Could it be that you are the Joshua, whom God is testing, so He can use you to tear down the walls of Jericho (i.e., the walls of depression, the walls of defeat; the walls of despair) in somebody's life?

Could it be that you are Hannah expecting to birth a son, but God is testing you, because He's about to birth a nation through you?

Pass the test, my friend, so God can bring you into a place of abundance and release you into your destiny.

Psalms 66:10-12 says "For you have tried us, O God; you have refined us as silver is refined. You brought us into the net; you laid an oppressive burden upon our loins. You made men ride over our heads; we went through fire and through water, yet you brought us out into a place of abundance."

It is my prayer that you will evaluate your response to your latest test then answer this question: Can God release me to the general public or does He need to keep me in "beta,"' being tested in limited small groups, because I keep failing the test?

Scripture Reading:

2 Corinthians. 13:5
Test yourselves to see if you are in the faith; examine yourselves! Or do you not recognize this about yourselves, that Jesus Christ is in you—unless you fail the test.

Part Two: The Gift of Charity

One the best ways to cultivate a desire to help others is to practice being *purposely grateful* ourselves. Spending a little time each day focusing on the things we have to be grateful for improves all aspects of our lives. Think, for a moment, about a day in which you wake up and remember what you *already* have, the blessings you *already* have been given, the money you have *already* received, the things that you *already* earned, the love you have *already* found. Are you willing to share what you already have with others?

The "Gift of Charity" theme recognizes that we have all received gifts from God and we are each called to share those gifts with one another in gratitude. Let's express our gratitude for the ways we have been blessed by following Our Lord's example of sacrificing for others.

Without charity or the pure love of Christ, whatever else we accomplish matters little. With it, all else becomes vibrant and alive.

HELPING OTHERS

As much as we may not want to believe it, life is full of ups and downs. Especially in the day in which we live, people are suffering in great numbers. Many people, even those in the upper class who previously held good jobs and lived in nice homes, are suddenly finding themselves out of work and homeless. The shock of such a loss is devastating beyond belief, especially when it occurs through no fault of their own. As a result, paralyzing fear and doubt can shatter the self-image and even cause relationship problems within the family unit. Mates who originally tried to be compassionate and understanding may lose patience and start blaming one another.

Men, in particular, base their identity on what they do for a living, and they often fight depression when they can no longer provide for their families. Over time many struggle to even find the courage to send out resumes or to look for work in such a tight job market.

The emotional shock after the loss of a job or a home is devastating. And while some are blessed to have family to take them in, what happens when it takes too long to find another job and the pressure builds to the breaking point? Where do they go from there?

People under this kind of stress are often upset and difficult to deal with, and over time their hosts come to the end of their generosity. At times the host's own situation is tenuous and their budget can no longer handle the burden of more mouths to feed.

Many of those in this situation have been abandoned by past friends, and have nowhere to turn. Some feel like outcasts, rejected by a society that once welcomed them with open arms.

As believers, we have countless opportunities to share the love of Christ with those who feel hopeless and afraid of the future. Some who perhaps haven't yet lost jobs, but who see the handwriting on the wall.

God cares for the needy and the poor because they are precious to Him. If God feels so strongly about the poor and loves them so deeply, how can we ignore their plight? Scripture speaks often to the issue of how we are to treat the poor. We are not to turn a deaf ear or a blind eye to the truly needy, but should ask God for creative ways to minister to their needs to show them the love of God in action. Who, better than Christians, can offer hope to those in need?

To turn a deaf ear means to ignore when someone asks for something; to ignore a cry for help. How can you just turn a deaf ear to a person's cry for food and shelter? You can't.

If we are in a position to help, we should do what we can to donate to our local food banks and pantries, support homeless shelters, and even give to Christian organizations that feed the hungry. We can ask God to show us individual families we can love and pray for, perhaps even some in our own churches or neighborhoods. By sharing God's love we can make an impact that will last for eternity. What could you do to help the hurting? How can you offer healing and assistance to those who are hurting, and make a difference? By using your gift.

We each have a gift. We all have something to share. No matter where you are in life, no matter what your skills or resources, you can change your own life and the lives of people in need. All you have to do is start right now, right where you are, with what you have at this very moment.

Hebrews 13: 16 reads: "Do not forget or neglect to do kindness and good, to be generous and distribute and contribute to the needy [of the church as embodiment and proof of fellowship], for such sacrifices are pleasing to God." (AMP)

Scripture Reading:

Psalms 72:4
May he vindicate the afflicted of the people, save the children of the needy, and crush the oppressor.

Psalms 72:12
He will rescue the poor when they cry to him; he will help the oppressed, who have no one to defend them.

PRACTICE HOSPITALITY

A friend called me one day and asked me, "What do you do when strangling someone in the church is not an option?" My flesh wanted to say, *"Smack them."* But my spirit prevailed over my flesh and I responded by saying, "Practice hospitality."

It's no secret that the number one challenge of any faith-based organization (church, etc.) is "people issues"--God's people driving God's people crazy! But God gives us a remedy in His word. He says to "practice hospitality."

The word "hospitality" buzzes through our churches and congregations every Sunday. But what does it really mean? Being friendly to visitors? Saying "hello" to everyone after church? Having dinner with a few members after a gospel concert?

As believers, we are quite good at inviting people to dinner, greeting visitors, offering guests the parking spots next to the church door, providing informational brochures, as well as creating websites and banners that are inviting. There's no doubt these frontline efforts have helped to cultivate friendliness and warmth, drawing our attention to the strangers among us. But those things are just the first step in practicing hospitality. The next step beyond greeting is feeding.

God has given us food to share with a world that is hungry, even famished. Spiritual wanderers--those who are spiritually starved and denied show up at our doors, not because they like our buildings or even because they like us. They come because they are hungry. Hungry for forgiveness; hungry for peace; hungry for love; hungry for mercy, hungry for a new, abundant life; and hungry for God's Word.

God's hospitality offers spiritual food as well as physical. It demands that we go beyond sharing our personal feelings and share the solid food of God's Word. When we do this, we welcome strangers not just to church, but into God's life. We also demonstrate to our enemies God's preference for handling conflict, by using love. This is the transforming power of hospitality that should always point our friends and enemies to God.

Scripture is very clear on the subject of hospitality. Jesus Himself not only taught it, but more importantly, He lived it.

Hospitality as described in the Bible should reflect our love for the brethren, and all those whom God sends in our direction. It describes a genuine love for others who are not yet a part of the faith community; an outward focus, a reaching out to those not yet known, a love that motivates church members to openness and adaptability, willingness to change behaviors in order to accommodate the needs and receive the talents of newcomers. Beyond intention, hospitality practices the gracious love of Christ, respects the dignity of others, and expresses God's invitation to others, not our own. Romans 12:13 says to "Share with God's people who are in need. Practice hospitality." This scripture is so clear that it really needs no explanation.

Why does the bible call hospitality a "practice"? In our culture there is a powerful tendency to identify the term "to practice" with something an individual does. But it is a mistake to see hospitality as an isolated activity done by a single individual. In this case, the term "to practice" means to learn a tradition, one that is sustained over a lengthy period of time. A practice can be defined as participation in a cooperative activity that emerges from a complex tradition of interactions among many people sustained over a long period of time. In any given practice, we are participating in something much greater than ourselves.

Every believer should be hospitable. Hospitality is an important and essential part of the Christian life. It is a reflection of God's character and His heart.

To be hospitable we have to be filled with gratitude to God for his generosity to us; then we can surely welcome others with the same spirit of generosity that we have experienced. Sometimes it works the other way round. Either way, we are talking about the one generous spirit of hospitality and that is the Spirit of God.

When is the last time you had someone in your home? Brought them food or clothing? Offered to drive a friend somewhere?

Scripture Reading:

Hebrews 13:2
Do not neglect to show **hospitality** *to strangers, for by doing that some have entertained angels without knowing it. (NRS)*

Romans 12:10-13
Be kindly affectionate to one another with brotherly love, in honor giving preference to one another; not lagging in diligence, fervent in spirit, serving the Lord; rejoicing in hope, patient in tribulation, continuing steadfastly in prayer; distributing to the needs of the saints, given to **hospitality.**

GOD GIVES

What would you do if you had a million dollars? Spend most of it! What about giving? Would you give it away? You know--to other people, to your church, to charity? You're probably saying, "Are you serious?"

That's a common response to the suggestion of giving. Unfortunately, even many Christians are that way. What about you? Do you regularly give a portion of your money back to God? If not, why not?

Jesus tells us to give–to give to everyone (Luke 6:30); to give hoping for nothing in return (verse 35); to give in the generous way God, who is kind to the unthankful and evil, gives (verse 35); and to care for others by giving. (See verse 38.) You and I can learn to give in this way, to overflow with care for others.

We have so much to give. We can give a smile, a greeting; an encouraging word, a touch, praise, thanks, good deeds, a note of appreciation and a hug.

When God asks us to give and to sacrifice, He is asking us to become more like Him, because He is a giver. There is no worthier goal than to be like God and to give the way He gives.

God has given us everything. He gives to us constantly. He is the giver of every good and perfect gift (James 1:17). Whether it is wisdom, peace, joy, friendship, prosperity or salvation itself, God is the giver of all good things. God gives.

God gives lovingly. It's out of love that God gives. God gives out of love to the point that He gives at a cost to Himself. "For God so loved the world that he gave his one and only son, that whoever believes in him shall not perish, but have eternal life" (John 3:16). God loves so God gives. That means that if we are going to give like God we give out of love.

God gives sacrificially. "For even the son of man did not come to be served, but to serve and to give his life as a ransom for many" (Mark 10:45). Giving is something that is so amazing that it costs God something to do it. God doesn't surround himself and say, "I will give, but only if it doesn't cost anything." God gives sacrificially. And if we are going to give like God, it means that we are called to giving beyond what's merely convenient and comfortable; whether it be of our time, our skills, or our money. Sacrificial love, sacrificial giving is giving beyond what we immediately receive back for ourselves.

Giving is a kingdom principle; giving brings even more blessing to the giver than to the recipient. Acts 20:35 (NIV) says "... 'It is more blessed to give than to receive." We are blessed when we give.

In a famous quote Winston Churchill said, "We make a living by what we get, we make a life by what we give." Don't just give, but give liberally, cheerfully, bountifully, lovingly and sacrificially. Proverbs 11:25 tells us, "The generous soul will be made rich." I am learning to be more generous.

Scripture Reading:

Deuteronomy 8:18
*And you shall remember the Lord your God, for it is He who **gives** you power to get wealth, that He may establish His covenant which He swore to your fathers, as it is this day.*

Psalms 146:7
*Who executes justice for the oppressed, Who **gives** food to the hungry. The Lord **gives** freedom to the prisoners.*

LOVE COVERS A MULTITUDE OF SINS

Jesus was a master of diplomacy. While knowing exactly the kind of people He was confronting He let love cover their sins, never exposing or humiliating anyone—ever. And not only that, but He also had a knack of gently confronting their sins in private and showing them a better way. In that way, He showed that while God is not fooled nor does He wink at our transgressions, He does not want to condemn us. In fact, He offers a remedy that transforms us. That remedy is forgiveness.

Do we as believers make a habit of covering the sins of others, the way Jesus did?

What does it mean "to cover?" The thought is--to hide from view. It does not mean--to look the other way. It does not mean--to patiently bear the sins. It does not mean--to ignore the sins. It means "to cover."

Remember the story of the woman taken in adultery? (John 8.) The crowd was ready to stone her, but Jesus leaned down and actually confronted the crowd when He wrote in the dirt the names and sins of those ready to cast stones, so that they dropped their stones and left Him alone with the woman. What an incredible picture of the way God covers us, even when we've been caught in sin.

Scripture says they will know us by our love. (1 John 4:16.) Envision what that means in real life. Have you ever had to go and apologize to another church member whose feelings you hurt? Have you ever had to forgive another church member who hurt your feelings? Have you ever had to help out a church member who never did anything for you and probably isn't about to?

Could the scripture also mean choosing to let go of revenge against the guy who cuts you off in traffic, even someone extremely rude and obnoxious? Could it mean setting aside anger when someone takes credit for work you've done on the job?

That's not to say that some things don't need to be gently confronted, but Scripture also says that a soft answer turns away wrath.

I'm convinced that as time passes and darkness deepens, the light of this kind of love will shine brighter than ever. But it will only be possible as we remember the grace, that is, the unmerited favor God bestowed on us when we least deserved it. If we keep that in mind we will be able to more easily extend it to others, and thereby let our light so shine before men, that they may see our good works, and glorify our Father which is in heaven.

Scripture Reading:

1 Peter 4:8
*Above all, love each other deeply, because **love** covers over a multitude of sins. (NIV)*

Part Three: The Gift of Faith

Faith is not about us. It is about God in us.

Faith begins with a belief in God that is rewarded with an attitude, a spirit within us, a feeling of incredible confidence, and a feeling of undefeatable victory in our circumstances. This feeling makes impossible huge mountains seem like miniature hills.

Faith is a gift from God. Because it is a gift, we cannot earn it, borrow it, buy it, and demand it. We must simply recognize that we can do mighty things in the kingdom of God if we would only put it to work.

Don't Give Up!

Ever heard it said, "Something's gotta give?" In spite of the bad grammar, we all know what it means. Our inner man is saying, "This is too much for me, God. I can't take it anymore. If it isn't one thing it's another, and if something doesn't give, I'm going to give up!"

I'm writing today to tell you not to give up. In the same way the devil often surprises you with unexpected trials and circumstances, God has a surprise for the devil. The surprise is your breakthrough--your miracle. However, the key to receiving your miracle is to hold on to God's Word and to stay the course.

Can I testify on this subject? You bet I can. My life is a sermon based on Genesis 50:20. "As for you, you thought evil against me, but God meant it for my good." Every plan, trap, scheme and plot the devil launched against me, God stood up as my advocate and turned it for my favor. I have to admit that while I often wept in grief and desperation in the middle of the situation, I refused to cease my praise. Even when the pain seemed unbearable I held onto my joy through the trials, because I had come to realize who God is.

Just who is God? The answer to this question is the foundation upon which we develop an intimate relationship with God, personally relating to Him. I am reminded of the words written in Daniel 11:32b, "… but the people who know their God will display strength and take action." And although no single statement could possibly explain all that God is, I want to remind you that God exists and that He is real. Everything He speaks, He does. Everything He promises, He keeps. The Bible says in Numbers 23:19: "God is not a man, that He should lie, nor a son of man, that He should repent. Has He said, and will He not do? Or has He spoken, and will He not make it good?"

Despite what you're going through, what has God spoken to you lately? What has He promised you? In case you can't recall, let me help you out. He said….

Yea, though (you) walk through the valley of the shadow of death, (you) will fear no evil: for I am with you. (Psalms 23:4, author paraphrase.)

I know you're hurting, but "trust me in this and see if I will not throw open the floodgates of heaven and pour you out so much blessing that you will not have room enough for it" (Malachi 3:10).

I know you don't understand why the enemy has attacked your life, but "who then can understand the thunder of my power?" (Job 26:14a). But I want you to rejoice and count this trial as joy. (James 1:3.) Because regardless to what the enemy has done, "I am the Lord and mighty in power" (Psalms 147:5).

Therefore, "Do not be afraid. Stand firm and you will see the deliverance that I will bring you today" (Exodus 14:13). For I, the Lord your God, is the one who goes with you to fight for you against your enemies to give you victory" (Deuteronomy. 20:4). Don't give up my child, "trust in my unfailing love (Psalms 13:5)" for you, because "as surely as I am the LORD, I will deliver you out of all trouble" (2 Samuel 4:9). "For I am the God who performs miracles" (Psalms 77:14).

God will personally ensure that every word and every promise He has ever given, is fulfilled in your life. Why? Because He has attached an oath to His promises. Hebrews 6:17 says: "Thus God, determining to show more abundantly to the heirs of promise the immutability of His counsel, confirmed it by an oath." To further prove how serious God is, He allowed Jesus' blood, death and resurrection to be a seal over everything He has promised. The Bible confirms that in Jesus, all the promises God has ever given, have their "Yes" and "Amen." (2 Corinthians 1:20)

My friend, enter this day not in trembling but in triumph! The fact that you are a believer means that you will suffer because all who desire to live godly in Christ Jesus will suffer persecution" (2 Tim. 3:12). But in the midst of your ordained suffering and trial, know that God is moving even in the emptiest and darkest places of your life and will lead you to victory. Second Corinthians 2:14 says that God always "leads us in triumph."

I know you don't understand why God chose you for the trial you're facing right now, but He does. He knew that in His strength you could pass the test before you even knew the test existed. The point is: God is fully aware of where He has ordered your steps, and your way of escape has already been made.

God is your Vindicator, and when the appointed time comes, your victory will come. Consider these facts:

- During its first year, Coca-Cola only sold 400 bottles of coke.
- NBA basket-baller Michael Jordan was cut from his high school basketball team.
- Dr. Seuss was rejected by 23 publishers before the 24th took on his books.
- Babe Ruth held the record for the most strike outs. He went on to also hold the record for the most home runs.
- Abraham Lincoln ran for public office several times and was defeated. He did not give up and was finally elected President of the United States of America.

The key is in not giving up. Unfortunately, people are throwing in the towel at record levels. They are throwing in the towel on their relationships and at their jobs. It seems like nobody can keep a commitment all the way to the end. I want to be different. How about you? What will it take to make it all the way to the end with Jesus?

Scripture Reading:

James 5:10-11
Take, my brethren, the prophets, who have spoken in the name of the Lord, for an example of suffering affliction, and of patience. Behold , we count them happy which endure . Ye have heard of the patience of Job, and have seen the end of the Lord; that the Lord is very pitiful, and of tender mercy.

I John 5:4
*For whatever is born of God overcomes the world. And this is the **victory** that has overcome the world--our faith.*

It's Closer Than It Appears

When driving a vehicle, you must use extreme caution when judging your distance from other cars while using the passenger side mirror. The passenger side mirror is quite different from the driver's side mirror. In most late model cars, the passenger side mirror has a sticker that reads "Caution: objects may be closer than they appear." This statement is posted on the mirror as a warning to drivers that the other car is not as far away as it appears.

Too often in the body of Christ, we move into a *parked position* (giving up) or a *changing lane position* (considering doing something else) when God has not answered our prayer according to our timetable. We pray for something to happen, and because we don't see evidence in the natural, we begin to think God is not going to honor what we've asked Him to do. But I want to tell you to hold on. Your answer is much closer than it appears.

The Apostle Paul defines faith as "being sure of what we hope for and certain of what we do not see." (Hebrews 11:1) Of course, the biggest problem for most of us is that we tend to base everything on what our five senses (hear, sight, smell, taste, touch) tell us. And since the spirit realm is not subject to any of these, our faith is often weak and impotent. As a result, we begin to doubt our all-powerful God.

Do you remember the story of Elisha in 2 Kings 6:8-23? Elisha found himself in a situation where he was completely surrounded by enemy troops, yet he remained calm and relaxed. His servant, however, must have been climbing the walls at the sight of such a hostile army of vicious-looking warriors and innumerable battle-ready chariots on every side.

Undaunted, Elisha said to him: "Don't be afraid. Those who are with us are more than those who are with them" (2 Kings 6:16). Elisha then prayed, "'O Lord, open his eyes so he may see." Then the Lord opened the servant's eyes, who then saw the hills full of horses and chariots of fire all around Elisha" (2 Kings 6:17). God was protecting Elisha and his servant with a whole army of magnificent angelic beings!

The reason Elisha did not panic is because He believed God had answered his prayer. Elisha was "sure of what he hoped for and certain of what he did not see" (Hebrews 11:1). Unlike many Christians today, Elisha was not a slave to the visible and the tangible. And he certainly wasn't a slave to the lies and deceptive practices of the enemy. This is the kind of faith believers must possess.

Just as God answered Elisha prayer, He will answer your prayer. So hang in there, your blessing is much closer than it appears. Therefore, I encourage you not to become "weary in well doing: for in due season you shall reap, if you faint not" (Galatians 6:9).

Release your faith, and watch God perform His Word for you. Your answer is much closer than appears.

Scripture Reading:

Galatians 6:9
And let us not grow weary while doing good, for in due season we shall reap if we do not lose heart. (NKJV)

Your Faith, Not the Law, is Moving God

There are times in our lives when we struggle because we do not see God moving, or at least not in the direction we wanted. And when times are hard we often let go of faith, and tend to bargain with God, trying to get Him to do what we want.

At times like these it's important to remember who God is. He is not a marionette whose strings we control. And He does not respond to our commands. Rather He is our Father, the one who created us and knows us inside and out. He understands how we think and what makes us feel insecure. He bottles our tears and keeps track of the numbers of hairs on our heads.

God created us for relationship and intimacy, but when things are hard we often walk away from closeness and just ask Him to give us the ten rules, because it's less complicated to do that than to cultivate relationship, especially when we're in trouble.

And because we can't see the road ahead it can be difficult to trust God when things are hard, which is why He told the children of Israel to take comfort by reminding themselves of the times when He came through for them in the past. (See Deuteronomy 8:2.)

When trials come, in order to restore a sense of control, we're often tempted to walk away from faith and pick up the law, reverting back to the legalism from which we were delivered as if it were a magic formula or a vending machine that would dispense answers at the touch of a button. In essence, convincing ourselves to believe, "If I do this, then God will do this."

Instead faith says, "I will choose to trust You, God, rather than focus on what I see with my eyes. I will wait on You for the right timing and choose not to go off on my own when I'm afraid. I will cast all my cares on You, knowing You care for me and will work out this situation for my good and Your glory."

That's the kind of faith that moves God so that He inclines His ear and moves on our behalf. In fact when we begin to praise God in faith and leave the door open for Him to move as He sees fit, before we see our answers,

God gets excited. Just as a human father whose child chooses to say, "I know it's going to be okay, because my daddy will take care of everything," you and I need to be as little children and let God be God.

God loves us with tender compassion, and that kind of love casts out fear, so that we no longer have to live by the law. (1 John 4:18.) Fall in love with Jesus again and cultivate that relationship, so that your faith will cast down fear and allow you to hold onto your liberty, for it is your faith, not the law, that moves God.

Scripture Reading:

Galatians 5:1
So Christ has really set us free. Now make sure that you stay free, and don't get tied up again in slavery to the **law**. *(NLT)*

Cast Your Bread Upon The Waters

Have you ever spent ten minutes arguing with a friend over who would pay the tip at a restaurant, or over the price of a gallon of milk that you wanted to give? I decided to write on this subject after witnessing both incidents during a trip to the grocery store.

If we understood the principle that one cannot give without receiving, we wouldn't quibble over a few dollars. We would graciously accept what someone wants to do for us or give us because we'd know that our friend would be blessed over and above what was given. Now I'm not advocating being a free-loader or letting other people pay your way all the time, but if someone insists upon giving you something, don't deny them the blessing of giving!

I have come to love the wisdom of Ecclesiastes. Chapter 11, in particular, is a rich tutorial on the principle of sowing and reaping, otherwise known as the Law of the Harvest, or in the vernacular, "What goes around comes around." The Law of the Harvest has taught me that if we expect to receive, we must first give. We have to make room for the things we seek before we can receive the new things we desire.

Ecclesiastes 11:1 explains, "Cast thy bread upon the waters: for thou shalt find it after many days. Give a portion to seven, and also to eight; for thou knowest not what evil shall be upon the earth." In other words, put out good, help others, and it will return to you in your hour of need. If you have sown good seeds, then in your moment of crisis, it will return to your rescue in the exact moment that you need it.

Whatever you put out, by eternal law, has to come back to you. Ecclesiastes emphasizes the certainty of this principle with two comparisons in verse 3. "If the clouds be full of rain, they empty themselves upon the earth: and if the tree fall toward the south, or toward the north, in the place where the tree falleth, there it shall be." The first comparison is: As surely as heavy clouds give rain and we find the tree where it fell, we will reap what we've sown. The second comparison is: As you find the tree where it fell, will you reap what you have sown.

There is a time to sow and a time to reap, but you don't do both at the same time. You can't be certain when or where you'll reap, but reap you shall.

Most likely the person to whom you give will not be the one to return your kindness. This is where most people stumble. They think they have to get back from the exact person to whom they gave, but that simply isn't the way this law works.

Ecclesiastes 11:4 says: "He that observes the wind shall not sow; and he that regards the clouds shall not reap." In truth the scripture means those who are so preoccupied with only what they can see--their current circumstances--will not put forth the effort to sow or to reap. The fact that they can't see how they're going to benefit will discourage them so that they do absolutely nothing. Because they will not sow, they cannot reap.

As believers, our job is to plant good seeds, and God will take care of the rest. Verse 5 compares the mystery of this principle to a child growing inside a mother's womb: "As thou knowest not what is the way of the spirit, nor how the bones do grow in the womb of her that is with child: even so thou knowest not the works of God who maketh all."

God takes what we sow and transforms it into abundance. Just as a tiny bean seed yields a plant laden with beans, so the Lord takes our efforts and multiplies them on our behalf. We can never be certain which seeds we sow will yield a harvest, but verse 6 admonishes us, "In the morning sow thy seed, and in the evening withhold not thine hand: for thou knowest not whether shall prosper, either this or that, or whether they both shall be alike good."

The simple interpretation of Verse 6 is that you should cheerfully do all within your power to lift, to build, to help and to serve from morning until evening, because you never know when or how your blessings shall return.

When you have something you no longer need, don't sell it. Give it away. If you sell it, the money will be all you receive in exchange. But if you give it away, it will come back to you in a far greater way. Jesus taught, "Give, and it shall be given unto you; good measure, pressed down, and shaken together, and running over, shall men give into your bosom. For with the same measure that ye mete withal it shall be measured to you again" (Luke 6:38).

If you want a new couch, call the Salvation Army to pick up the one you have. If you want new clothes, clean out your closet and give your old ones to a charity. Make room for the things you desire by giving away the old and making room for the new. Don't be afraid that you won't receive. By law you have to.

Today, I challenge you to step out on faith and try an experiment. Pick something from around your house that you would like to replace. Give it away and see what God brings you in its place. I think you'll be pleasantly surprised.

Scripture Reading:

Ecclesiastics. 11:1
Cast thy bread upon the waters: for thou shalt find it after many days.

Part Four: Gift of Family

Nearly a decade ago the White House Conference on Children issued this statement: "America's families are in trouble - trouble so deep and pervasive as to threaten the future of our nation." At that conference, Paul Popenoe of the American Institute of Family Relations stated: "No society has ever survived after its family life deteriorated. If the family fails, then all the other institutions of society will fail. The family is the basic unit of society under-girding all else."

Repeatedly in Ephesians 5:21 through Ephesians 6:4 Paul gives the key to having a family based on God's plan. "Wives, be subject to your own husbands, as to the Lord" (5:22). "Husbands, love your wives, just as Christ loved the church and gave Himself up for her" (5:24). "Children, obey your parents in the Lord" (6:1). "Fathers... bring them up in the discipline and admonition of the Lord" (6:4). The key to all family functioning is having God and Jesus at the center.

The family is a gift from God.

What's In Your Mouth?

I met a young girl who seemed to have a lot going for her but consistently failed in many areas of her life. As hard as I tried I could not understand why she chose failure over a successful, happy life. She was beautiful, talented and intelligent, but it was obvious that she did not esteem herself. And she continually made bad choices.

For months, I struggled to understand why she could not see her true value as a person, that is--until I met her mother. Her mother saw her as the biggest failure ever born and told her so. She would criticize her daughter to anyone who would listen. In her daughter's presence she would announce to a roomful of people what a failure she was. It did not take great discernment to see why the girl struggled so. Why should she like herself when the woman who gave birth to her saw nothing good in her own child?

The girl told me that as soon as she was old enough she ran away from home and began living with an older man. Unfortunately, her mind had been poisoned by the seeds of self-hatred her mother had planted from birth.

I believe this is what Proverbs 14:1 means when it says, "The wise woman builds her house, but with her own hands the foolish one tear hers down." The mother's physical house was in excellent condition, but the heritage she passed down to her child was devastating, and as a result the girl lived a very destructive lifestyle.

In recent years I've counseled many young men and women who struggled with incredible self-hatred. In time they shared that such feelings began early in life when authority figures spoke down to them, humiliating and denigrating them.

It's important to realize that words are more powerful than most of us understand. They have the potential to uplift of tear down, either breathing life into one's spirit, or eroding the sense of well-being. Proverbs 18:21 says: "The tongue has the power of life and death." The power of the tongue is great, capable of producing life or death depending on how it's used.

Our words influence the way we act and feel as well as determine our attitude and outlook on life. That's right, the tongue is a powerful weapon and our words are its ammunition. What we believe in our hearts comes out of our mouths and will determine our future.

The Book of Proverbs has much to say about our tongues. In the end they hold the keys to life. However, what comes out of our mouths is the result of what we have put in our hearts. Proverbs 21:23 says, "Whoso keepeth his mouth and his tongue keepeth his soul from troubles."

The words we speak reveal a great deal about us--our attitudes, beliefs, feelings, and expectations. Our words not only communicate what we want others to hear, but they have the power to influence and make a real impact on people and situations.

I've noticed that when positive Christians come together, they tend to have positive desires, take positive actions and produce positive results. Positive people encourage and support one another. Negative people, on the other hand, tend to think negatively, take negative actions and produce negative results.

Love people with the words you speak. Speak well of your family, others, and especially of your children. Words spoken out of frustration or anger can wound a person's self-esteem, while words of affection, praise, encouragement and affirmation along with positive guidance will build his inner sense of worth and security.

Be careful what you put in your mouth and what you speak with your mouth. Mathew 12:34 says, "For out of the abundance of the heart the mouth speaks." When you speak what's in your heart you release it into your life or someone else's life. Remember, a man's level of success is set by his tongue. (See Proverbs 13:2.)

Scripture Reading:

Proverbs 25:11
A word fitly spoken is like apples of gold in pictures of silver.

LEAD YOUR CHILD IN WORSHIP

In our society families are swamped with time-consuming activities and many struggle to find time to do anything together. Studies have shown that though they'd rather die than admit it, children and youth are more powerfully impacted by their parents than by any other source. Not surprisingly their example speaks much louder than their words, which means parents have an incredible opportunity to model passion for Christ, from the time children are small. What better place than in a corporate worship setting? In case it's not obvious, this means parents and children should sometimes sit together. And if that's not possible, parents can have children sit in front of them where they can oversee their participation and observe their behavior.

In most church services, youth sit in back pews sleeping, texting, talking and playing while their parents worship elsewhere. Are they to blame? No. Unless trained otherwise, kids will be kids. Rather the responsibility rests on the parents. Proverbs 22:6 says, "Train up a child in the way he should go…" Parents should teach children the Word of God by precept and example. Teach them how to worship God in the beauty of holiness. Help them understand that church is a place to reverence God and give Him glory.

Children learn much more by example than by lectures or sermons. Taking your children to church is important. But if the home life is a poor example of faith, then all the lessons in the world, taught by all the best teachers, will fall on deaf ears. What takes place in your home will set in concrete the values your children adopt. Throughout Paul's discussion of marriage and childrearing (Eph. 5:21-6:4), he constantly refers to an atmosphere in which family members are protected. So a husband will not be threatened by a wife who submits (Eph. 5:22). So a wife will not be afraid of a husband who dies to self for his wife (Eph. 5:25) or who treats his wife as his own body (Eph. 5:28-29). So parents will not be pressured by kids who honor them (Eph 6:1) and children will not be angered by parents who nurture (Eph. 6:4). A family is to be a group of people who make it safe to live, to work, to worship, to succeed and to fail, without threat or intimidation or fear.

Researchers say there are several factors that contribute to the tendency for youth to turn to drugs, gangs, alcohol, pre-marital sex and other worldly vices. And unfortunately statistics prove that even children raised in Christian homes can have troubling behaviors. But these can be mitigated by parents who model their passion for Christ and their love and commitment to the goal of raising godly children.

As hard as it is to believe, it is possible to raise godly children. When we pray in faith and speak life words into their lives, blessing them and encouraging them to become all they can for the kingdom of God...When we help them envision being mightily used of God...When we pray a hedge of protection around them and plead the blood of Jesus over them, we can trust that God will be faithful to do His part and make them flourish in the courts of the Lord. (Psalms 92:12-16, Psalms 103:17-18.)

God established the family. God ordained that families would be the backbone of any and all societies. So take time to lead your child into worship, it will make a difference in society.

Scripture Reading:

Proverbs 22:6
Train a child in the way he should go, and when he is old he will not turn from it. (NIV)

CHILDREN--A GIFT FROM THE LORD

Motherhood is one of God's most precious blessings. It brings much joy and fills the heart with a new and special kind of love.

Even though the life of a mother is filled with love, joy, and all manner of happiness, it often contains fears and questions. At times, the demands can be overwhelming.

Are you a young mother exhausted from overwork, lack of sleep, a victim of noise overload and chaos? Does it seem like a thankless job, where the room you just cleaned is already filled with crushed crackers, broken toys and squabbling children? Does it seem like the laundry never ends and that no one is grateful for your efforts? Does it feel like what you're doing is making no spiritual impact for the kingdom? Well, take heart, sweet sister, because God sees your hard work, and He is pleased. He is saying, "Well done, thou good and faithful servant."

As hard as it may be to believe right now, the Lord says children are a gift, and your job is the most important one of all. Your godly input into your children's lives will count for eternity and may ultimately change the world. And though days may seem endless now, they are more fleeting than you know. One day soon you'll look back and realize it flew past before you knew it. That's one good reason to treasure every moment and look for things that make you smile. Like every other phase of life, this too shall pass.

In this day and age many women wait until they have the time and money to have children, while others decide to have no children at all. But God says children are important, like arrows in a quiver, protecting the future of the family. In fact, in Bible days, a Jewish woman who had no children was considered cursed, whereas the woman with many children was considered exceedingly blessed. Very different from the way the world looks at children today.

I love being a mother, and it has become a large part of my identity. Much of my parenting has been trial and error, guessing, working on instinct, doing the best at the moment, calling my mother and praying to God when all else failed. Many times my mother heard me utter, "I've never been a parent before. I'm doing the best I can and he still won't sleep all night." My mother would respond, "You are not expected to be experienced. You will become better with practice. In the meantime, nurture this little gift the best you know how."

This little gift was my first child, Steven. I begin to nurture, encourage and develop him according to his unique temperament and abilities. During the nurturing process, I discovered that children offer us clues to their gifts at a very early age through their temperaments, emotional responses, talents and intelligence. And because I did not deny Steven's individuality, later on in life I was able to ascertain his unique gift and genius.

Four-year old Steven asked me for a toy keyboard player for his birthday. He banged on that keyboard night and day. Within months, Steven told me he was going to be a famous piano player one day. As a young adult, Steven is on the path of becoming one of the world's greatest pianists. This example illustrates how each child's temperament, with its preferences, is present from birth.

Although raising my son was a daunting and overwhelming task at times, I was able to recognize the value of his boyhood (by staying in the presence of God) and now he's doing great work in the kingdom of God.

So no matter how crazy and chaotic it gets in your home, you can take back your peace and stay on top of the situation by staying in the presence of God. Suzannah Wesley, mother of famed evangelists John and Charles Wesley, had nineteen children, and as you can imagine her household was busy and overwhelming at times. But she made a habit of lifting her apron and putting it up over her head to signal the children that she needed time alone to be with God. And soaking in God's presence empowered her with self-control, patience, and strength for each day. That little habit kept her sane and, in the end, her sons won untold numbers of souls for Christ.

When you feel overwhelmed think of it this way: God says your job is the most important job in the world, and He highly esteems your skills. Your reward in heaven will be great if you choose to keep going when you feel like giving up. So never, never, never give up. Your children are gifts from God!

Scripture Reading:

Psalms 127:3
Children are a gift from the LORD; they are a reward from him. (NLT)

Isaiah 44:3
For I will pour water on him who is thirsty, And floods on the dry ground; I will pour My Spirit on your descendants, And My blessing on your offspring.

Restoring The Husband and Father to His Rightful Place

From the beginning of time God has called Himself our Father and described Himself as our protector, our provider, our comforter and our biggest cheerleader.

In the same way, the role of men as husbands and fathers is patterned after His example. They were created to marry and bear children, to love and protect them, and train them up in the nurture and instruction of the Lord. According to God's original plan fathers are to bless their children and encourage them to become stable, productive adults who glorify the Lord Jesus Christ and make their lives count for Him.

Over the past sixty to seventy years the role of men in society has dramatically changed. Women, who had previously been at home, began taking jobs in the war-time workforce and, without meaning to, became much more self-sufficient. And while there is nothing intrinsically wrong with self-reliance, over time women's education and income increased to where it slowly eliminated the need for the man's contribution. This, in turn eroded the man's identity and self-esteem, to the point that some have become passive and even depressed over their lack of purpose. Others have grown bitter and angry, displaced from their families, relegated to weekend visits with their children.

At the same time society's views toward marriage and divorce were radically changing so that, at this point in time no relationship is seen as permanent.

And while not many Christian teachers are bold enough to address this subject, let me say the children have suffered terribly from the absence of their fathers. Many children suffer long-term and even life-long feelings of rejection as a result of the father's absence. Young boys desperately need a male role model to learn what it means to be a male, and how to treat females. Girls of all ages need a father to make them feel secure and to model for them the qualities they should seek in a husband. In reality, the giant chasm left by the fathers' absence is one that will not easily be filled, especially in the hearts of their children.

Scripture is very specific on the role of the father. Families are made up of mothers, fathers and children born to the union, and were designed that way for a specific purpose, because if one of these elements is missing, the unit is incomplete and generally speaking, some needs, especially emotional needs, tend to go unmet. This is not to say there aren't occasional reasons for a family to split up, but that is not God's ideal.

To put it bluntly, it's time to restore men to their rightful place. They are a vital part of God's plan to fully bless the family, so that it fulfills God's plan to nurture healthy, secure and capable individuals able to model the Father-love of God to a lost and dying world.

Scripture Reading:

Genesis 17:5-7
Neither shall thy name any more be called Abram, but thy name shall be Abraham; a father of many nations have I made thee. And I will make thee exceeding fruitful, and I will make nations of thee, and kings shall come out of thee. And I will establish my covenant between me and thee and thy seed after thee in their generations for an everlasting covenant, to be a God unto thee, and to thy seed after thee.

Life Lessons From My Dad!

I often thank God for setting the example for me as a parent. There were times when I haven't listened, when I've done what I wanted to do, and He has chastened me. And while it hurt I learned valuable lessons.

God also used my father to teach me valuable lessons. My father lovingly disciplined me as a child so I would grow to be a responsible adult and to please God. No matter how difficult it was, he stood strong and chastised me with love.

It's been nine years since the Lord called my father home to glory. Yet despite my ongoing struggle to deal with life without him, it would be equally tragic not to acknowledge his impact on my life. So, in honor of my late father, Charlie Stewart, Jr., I would like to share some of the life lessons he taught me as a child.

In my father's words...

Know the difference between "needs" and "wants." True needs are few and include: food, shelter and clothing. Almost everything else is a "want" and can be delayed.

Be prepared. Stop spending all of your money the first time the ice cream truck stops by. The ice cream truck comes by our house every day. If you learn this principle as a kid you will apply it to your adult finances. You never know when unexpected home or car repairs will pop up, so it's wise to think ahead. Scripture says a wise man plans for the future (Proverbs 21:20), so if you stash money away for emergencies you'll never be caught unprepared.

Be generous. You are blessed if you grew up with two parents who love you, to have a roof over your head and enough food to eat and warm clothes to wear. Not everyone is as blessed as you are so be generous toward others. Give away some of what you have to others who need it more, especially if you haven't used it in awhile.

Know how much you spend. As a child you spend money on candy and gum. Later in life you'll spend money on housing, gas, food and clothes. Knowing how much you spend, and on what, lets you make good choices.

Refuse to live your life on someone else's terms. Live your own life. And don't let anyone dictate who you become, but God.

Trust God. You will never be wiser than God, but you can be wiser than others, if, when you lack wisdom, you ask God.

To all the men who believe in the *power of instruction* and take time to inspire and teach their children. Your investment will last a lifetime.

My father passed away June 26, 2001. He was a remarkable good man. He was a person of devotion and integrity, a man who understood a hard day's work. His core accomplishment was family. He poured vast amounts of love and energy into his nine children during our most formative years. The loss of my father has been painful, yet also strangely reaffirming because it has made me ever more aware of the rewards of having him as my dad. Perhaps the most consoling words came from my mother: "Think of the legacy he left you -- a hunger for knowledge, a great childhood, an example of a life whose riches owe little to money, a sense that anything is possible if you work hard, a model of what a real father should be. Those are all great gifts."

Scripture Reading:

Proverbs 1:5
A wise man will hear and increase learning, And a man of understanding will attain wise counsel. (NKJV)

Proverbs 22:6
Train up a child in the way he should go, And when he is old he will not depart from it.

"Because I Said So..." (For this is right)

I grew up in the "Because I said so" era. And once when I was a little girl my mother gave me an order and when I asked "why?" I was knocked to the floor. It only took one "knock-down" for me to understand that when Jessie Stewart (my mom) gave an order, I needed to comply.

Children often ask their parents, "Why" when their parents give them commands they need to obey. What parent hasn't answered this exasperating question with the now-famous phrase, "Because I said so"? As much as we hated that phrase as kids, we as parents often pull it out as the trump card. I have come to believe that, at times, it's the perfect answer.

Ephesians 6:1 says: "Children, obey your parents in the Lord, for this is right." Doesn't that sound very much like the phrase, "Because I said so?" Here God gives us the divine "because I said so" with the phrase "for it is right." Some things are right, whether we understand why or not, while some things are just wrong whether we understand why or not. God is like a parent. When He gives a command, He doesn't usually explain why. He simply expects obedience, for our own good.

Often we are not obedient because we do not understand that God has set up certain rules to protect us and work for our benefit. If we choose to live outside the arena of obedience, then spiritual darkness and confusion have access to our lives. When we obey, life is simple and clear and offers unlimited blessings.

God delights in a Christian who is compliant, cooperative, and responsive to Him and His commands.

The Bible says that Noah was given new life because he did *all* that God asked him to do. (Genesis 6:22). The minute we start walking in obedience, God offers us opportunities for new life. The minute we start to think it's not necessary to obey, we have opened the door for spiritual darkness. Remember, "He who obeys instructions guards his life" (Proverbs 19:16 NIV).

This article honors all of the "Because I said so" Moms out there. Because of you, your son or daughter understands, just like me, that it is wiser to bow in submission to God than to question His actions.

To those of you who have *not* experienced motherhood, I pray that you will use the gift of God's Word to properly advise others. Teach them the truth about obedience to God—and give a gift that really counts.

Scripture Reading:

Ephesians 6:1
Children, obey your parents in the Lord, for this is right.

Exodus 20:12
Honor your father and mother. Then you will live a long, full life in the land the LORD your God will give you. (NLT)

Part Five: Gift of Forgiveness

I love what Dr. Charles Stanley wrote in his book *"The Gift of Forgiveness."* He said forgiveness is "the act of setting someone free from an obligation to you that is a result of wrongdoing against you. A person who has an unforgiving spirit is always the real loser, much more so than the one against whom the grudge is held."

The inability or refusal to forgive has become one of the greatest destructive elements in the world. We hold grudges. We seek revenge. We find ourselves trapped in anger, resentment, spite and hostility–emotions that poison both our own lives and our relationship with others. Time and time again, our ability to move forward is short circuit by memory of past wrongs held dear.

Forgiveness is a gift from God. Forgiveness is a gift to oneself. Forgiving does not undo what has been done. But it is an act of self-love; a healing gift we give ourselves and others.

The Bondage of Guilt

Scripture says we have been saved, transformed by the forgiveness of our sins. But if that's true why do we so often struggle with feelings of condemnation?

Many people raised in churches have been erroneously taught on this subject. Somehow, though they grasp the concept of being saved by faith, they believe that their works, their performance is what keeps them in God's good graces.

Nothing can be further from the truth. The reality is this: God knows we are weak, and does not expect perfection from mere human beings. Never has—never will. That's why He said, "Apart from Me you can do nothing." (John 15:5.) And conversely He says, (author paraphrase) "You can do all things through Christ who strengthens you." (Phillippians 4:13.)

In our own strength we are truly helpless. Without Him we are no different than we've always been, because our flesh is still carnal. But in Him we are new creations. That's why it takes the continual renewing of our minds, to transform us over time, into His likeness.

And until we realize we must die to our flesh daily and let Him live through us, we will continue to struggle with sin that won't let us go. Not because He isn't willing, but because we refuse to believe it.

However, the other half of that equation is this: Once we've been saved, God actually forgets our sins, and doesn't remember them at all until and unless we bring them up. Therefore, it's up to us to take God at His word and live as if we are what He says we are—the very redeemed of the Lord, empowered by the Holy Spirit of God Himself whose DNA actually indwells us. That's an incredible thought, isn't it?

So when you feel condemned by guilt and feelings of failure, tell the devil this: "I am redeemed of the Lord, bought by His blood, in right standing with God. And there is therefore now no condemnation to them that are in Christ Jesus, including me. So I render you and your lies harmless in Jesus' name. I can do all things through Christ who strengthens me." Then choose to rejoice with all your heart and soul and strength, believing what He says about you, and watch Him transform your life into the powerhouse He intended it to be.

Scripture Reading:

Romans 8:1-2

There is therefore now no condemnation to those who are in Christ Jesus, who do not walk according to the flesh, but according to the Spirit. For the law of the Spirit of life in Christ Jesus has made me free from the law of sin and death.

The Mechanics of Forgiveness

Forgiveness is an interesting concept though it's often a tough sell. That's because we as human beings tend to keep records of the wrongs others do to us, and sometimes those balance sheets weigh pretty heavily in our favor, as if there were points for being misused and abused. And while it's only human to do that, God wants to change that about us, so that we live above the level of mere humanity.

I find it intriguing to know that from the beginning of time God knew we would fail, and yet He chose to create us anyway. And while we were still in sin He invited us into His family where He forgave our sins, (even the ones we hadn't committed yet), changed our character, and began to gently mold us, little by little, into His likeness.

Too often people forget that forgiveness has two parts. If we want to reap all the benefits of God's forgiveness and the forgiveness of others, we have to be willing to grant it to others.

In the real world, the concept of unforgiveness can be compared to conjoined twins, where one dies and the other is left carrying around a dead body, a toxic load that will eventually poison him too, one system at a time, and ultimately end, his very life. The truth is that bitterness and unforgiveness have a way of actually eating us up from the inside out, like a cancer gone out of control.

Forgiveness can be a challenge, though, because it requires us to give up control, to give up the need for payback, for revenge. And in some ways that's the toughest sacrifice of all, because we feel we'll be stripped of what little power we have if we forgive. But that too, is a misconception, because there is truly no one more free and carefree, than the one who has freely forgiven another.

Forgiving someone is, in essence, cutting the ties that bind us to earth so that we can soar in the spirit, far above what we could otherwise do, so there is nothing between us and God, and absolutely nothing hindering His plan in our lives--nothing we can't accomplish. What an amazing way to live!

Scripture Reading:

Matthew 6:14-15
If you forgive those who sin against you, your heavenly Father will forgive you. But if you refuse to forgive others, your Father will not forgive your sins. (NLT)

Mark 11:25
And whenever you stand praying, if you have anything against anyone, forgive him, that your Father in heaven may also forgive you your trespasses.

LETTING GOD STEP INTO OUR SHOES

There's something remarkable, almost magical about the process of forgiveness. Once we make the choice to forgive it takes the outcome out of our hands and puts it in God's hands, so that He is ultimately responsible and can turn things around in the most amazing ways. It means stepping out of our shoes, knowing that when our hearts are right we are in the holy presence of God. And when we bow before Him, we give Him permission to step into our shoes, knowing we've already done all we can do. If our hearts are right we truly won't want the other person to be cursed; rather we'll want them to be saved and changed just as we were. And the interesting thing is, when we're in this place, God loves to surprise us with remarkable blessings as a reward for choosing to let go of our need for retribution.

Have you ever been defrauded or badly wounded by a friend or a loved one and you had to decide whether to hold a grudge or let it go--even for something huge, like molestation or grand theft? These things are, by law, prosecutable, which might give us license to hold onto control. But what's God's take on the issue?

He says that justice belongs to Him. And He actually honors us when we step out of our shoes to let Him step in and take control of the situation. There are even bonus benefits to doing such things. Once we don't carry it anymore we can rest knowing that He will do what is right for both parties. And lest we believe otherwise, because He is love, He will never take lightly an offense done to us. Instead He actually comforts us, weeping with us over the terrible harm done. But then He does something remarkable. He touches and heals us and then turns around for our good what our enemy meant for harm.

Our God is trustworthy to take up the cause on our behalf and use it for His glory, if we can just let go. Scripture says letting go and letting God is like pouring coals of fire on someone's head. In other words, convicting them of the wrong they have done, entirely without our involvement. It's an incredible way to live. If you will choose to do things God's way I think you'll find that, indeed, His burden is light--nearly weightless.

Scripture Reading:

Ephesians 6:13
Therefore put on the full armor of God, so that when the day of evil comes, you may be able to stand your ground, and after you have done everything, to stand. (NIV)

Part Six: Gift of God

Christ is the visible image of the invisible God. He existed before God made anything at all and is supreme over all creation. Christ is the one through whom God created everything in heaven and earth. He made the things we can see and the things we can't see— kings, kingdoms, rulers, and authorities. Everything has been created through him and for him. He existed before everything else began, and he holds all creation together. (Colossians 1:15-17 NLT)

Yet as much as we view the coming of Jesus as God's greatest gift to us, God views the incarnation from a different perspective. Jesus comes to earth to give the Father a gift. This story is for us, but it is not about us. It is about Him. It is about our Father's love and grace. It's about our Father wanting us back so badly that He sent his Son to buy us back. Jesus came to give us as a gift back to God. He came to redeem us, to reclaim us, and to bring us home to His Father.

Christ's great gift to us was His life and sacrifice. Should that not then be our small gift to Him. God's desire is that we receive His perfect gift--His son, Jesus, and share that gift with others.

John Called Him "The Word"

Why do you suppose Jesus was called "the Word"? One way to answer that question is to ponder what else He might have been called and why that would have been inadequate compared to the title "the Word." For example, He could have been *called* "the Deed": "In beginning was the deed and the deed was with God and the deed was God." One of the differences between a deed and the Word is that a deed is more ambiguous. Compared to our words, which are sometimes confusing and subject to various interpretations, our deeds are far more unclear and hard to pin down. That's why we so often explain ourselves with words. Words capture the meaning of what we do more clearly than the deeds themselves. God did many mighty deeds in history, but He gave a certain priority to the Word. One of the reasons, I think, is that He puts a high value on simple and straightforward communication.

Another example is that John might have called him "the Thought." "In the beginning was the Thought, and the Thought was with God and the Thought was God." But one of the differences between a thought and a word is that a word is generally pictured as moving outward from the thinker for the sake of establishing communication. I think John wanted us to conceive of the Son of God as existing both for the sake of communication between Him and the Father, and for the sake of appearing in history as God's communication to us.

John might also have called Him "the Feeling." "In the beginning was the Feeling, and the Feeling was with God and the Feeling was God." But again, I would say, feelings do not carry any clear conception or intention or meaning. Feelings, like deeds, are ambiguous and need to be explained--with words.

When Scripture called Jesus "the Word," it emphasized the fact that His very purpose was to bridge the vast communication gap between God and man. First, and foremost, He exists, and has always existed, from all eternity for the sake of communication with the Father. Secondarily, but infinitely more important for us, the Son of God became divine communication to us. One might say, in summary, that calling Jesus "the Word" implies that He is "God-Expressing-Himself."

The fact that God gave us "the Word" is evidence of His love for us. The term "revelation" simply means that God communicated to mankind what He is like and how we can have a right relationship with Him through His Word. These are things that we could not have known had not God divinely revealed them to us in "the Word." God's revelation of Himself in "the Word" contains everything man needs to know about God in order to have a right relationship with Him. If the Bible is truly the Word of God, and it is, then it is the final authority for all matters of faith, religious practice, and morals.

Skeptics have regarded "the Word" as mythological, but archeology has established it as historical. Opponents have attacked its teaching as outdated, but its moral and legal concepts and teachings have had a positive influence on societies and cultures throughout the world.

"The Word of God" continues to be attacked by science, psychology, atheist and political movements, and yet it remains just as true and relevant today as it was when it was first written. It is a book that has transformed countless lives and cultures. No matter how its opponents try to attack, destroy, or discredit it, "the Word" remains just as strong, just as true, and just as relevant after the attacks as it was before. Despite every attempt to corrupt, attack, or destroy it, "the Word" yet stands because it is supernaturally protected by God.

It should not surprise us that no matter how "the Word" is attacked, it always comes out unchanged, unaffected, unmoved, unbothered, unaltered, untouched and unscathed. After all, Jesus said, "Heaven and earth will pass away, but my words will never pass away" (Mark 13:31). After looking at the evidence one can say without a doubt that yes, the Bible is truly God's Word.

"The Word" says Jesus died on the cross to pay the price for sinners. What looked like a shameful death for Jesus was actually a glorious triumph for God's plan, because it is through the cross that Jesus won the ultimate victory over Satan, sin and death.

So let us who are in Christ Jesus begin sharing this precious gift with others. Sharing "the Word" with others is to be an overflow of love and expression from a life now in Christ.

Scripture Reading:

John 1:1
In the beginning was the Word and the Word was with God, and the Word was God.

God's Word--The Best Place To Stand

The world is speeding up--and it is taking us with it! Former generations never had to cope with the pressures we do.

Job insecurity and competition in the marketplace have everyone from factory workers to CEOs under pressure to produce. More and more people must hold down several jobs just to make ends meet--and the pressure doesn't stop when the workday ends. Needless to say, in some states the price of gasoline exceeds $6 per gallon. Commuters spend hours in nerve-wracking traffic or crowded public transit. If they are parents, they go home to challenges their own parents never even imagined. Students' future job opportunities (and happiness, they are told) depend on them mastering an ever-increasing mass of information and keeping up with technology that changes at a dizzying pace. Movies, TV, music and advertising have nearly everyone trying harder than ever to be richer, more glamorous, more successful, more powerful, and more famous. Who isn't stressed out these days?

And just in case we don't have enough problems of our own, we are constantly subjected to "secondhand stress." Friends, co-workers, hurried shoppers, depressed Christians, weary missionaries, burdened preachers, troubled saints and the driver behind us are often more than willing to share their stress with us. Those who are not living in the fast lane live in fear of being blown off the road by those who are. It seems there is no end to it!

But it doesn't have to be that way. There is a sure and simple cure that only takes a few minutes a day and doesn't cost a thing--no therapists, no drugs, no rigorous exercise routines, no rehab, no gadgets, and no gimmicks. And I can guarantee that by using this cure you'll feel better and be in better health, get more done and sleep better. You will be happier, have more joy, get more out of life and have more to give. Read, believe and stand on the faithful Word of God. Stand firm in it, on it and with it.

As humans, we become so accustomed to the ineffective nature of our words that we fail to appreciate the power that is wielded by God's words. Hebrews 1:3 says, "He upholds all things by the word of His power."

The Word of God is awesome power, an irresistible power that will not return to God without bearing fruit. God's words are powerful beyond our imagination. When you and I speak we merely warm the air a bit. But when God speaks the universe trembles. In Exodus 20 we see how God's thundering voice shook the very foundations of Mt. Sinai. The idea is that God's words are earth-shattering in their effect and cannot be ignored. We should keep that notion in mind when taking in God's words.

My friend, if we are to be delivered *"in times like these"* then we must come to see that God's communication to us in His Word is a mighty force that works on our behalf. Again-- read, believe and stand on God's Word. When you speak the Word of God, you are tapping into limitless power! When you speak and believe the Word of God, you can expect its infinite power to bring forth astounding results in every area of your life. When you help others believe the Word of God, you provide them with the instrument that will enable them to do things far beyond what is considered normal.

Scripture Reading:

Mark 13:31
Heaven and earth shall pass away : but my words shall not pass away.

God's Best Gift—Grace

What kind of love gives its life for an undeserving and unrepentant sinner? The incomprehensible love of God demonstrated by grace, also called *unmerited favor*. Such a notion is nearly unfathomable with our finite minds, because we think in terms of "deserving" or "undeserving" and give our favor accordingly. But God doesn't do that, does He?

Instead God saw mankind the way a father sees his child on whom he has lavished all his love, and placed all his hopes and dreams. Even when that child becomes wayward and rebellious, he loves him because he is his own flesh and blood and he waits and yearns for the day of their reconciliation. In the same way we are God's own flesh and blood, made in the image of God, for the purpose of relationship. And because God prized intimacy above all else, He offered tender compassion rather than condemnation when the human race fell into the clutches of sin.

In the beginning God created Adam and Eve for fellowship and designed the Garden of Eden to be a place where they could flourish. Everything was supplied, and all they had to do was enjoy the warm and loving company of God. But sin changed all that, so that God went to Plan B. Now because He is holy, He couldn't just condone or overlook their sin. Rather He had to come up with a way to deal with it that would not only hold up a standard of holiness but also demonstrate His love and "woo" them back into relationship.

The Old Testament answer to that problem was the system of sacrifices. Now if you've ever read the Book of Exodus you've seen how costly, arduous and messy the sacrificial system was. (Exodus 24.) During that time it took a tremendous amount of effort to have their sins covered, to keep their souls from eternal hell. Can you imagine it?

But Jesus was the New Testament answer to the problem of sin. God had His own Son, Jesus, exit heaven, and come to earth to be born as a human baby and grow up to be that one perfect, final sacrifice, that would not only cover the sins of mankind, but would also remove them as far as the east is from the west so they would no longer be held against us. Psalm 103:12 says it so beautifully: "As far as the east is from the west, so far has He removed our transgressions from us. Just as a father has compassion on his children, so the Lord has compassion on those who fear Him. For He Himself knows our frame; He is mindful that we are but dust."

And not only did He redeem us from the clutches of Satan, hell and death, but He did the unthinkable; He went so far as to adopt us into the royal family, the family of God, where He gives us special places of honor in the kingdom. And what's even more remarkable is that He sent His Holy Spirit to actually indwell and empower us to walk in newness of life. His Spirit, from that point on, never ever leaves us again. And with the Holy Spirit inside us, God enables us to do even greater, more astounding things than even Jesus did.

That kind of love should get us excited enough to jump up and down and praise and worship God with all our hearts, souls, minds and strength. Such knowledge should transform us. Join me in meditating on the incredible grace of God and give Him thanks, letting the fire of passion be stirred up inside us. For in the process, He promises we will never be the same again.

Scripture Reading:

Romans 5:8
But God demonstrates his own love for us in this: While we were still sinners, Christ died for us. (NIV)

Part Seven: Gift of Healing

One of the questions asked by many Christians is, "Why do some people get healed and others don't?" Jesus told His disciples to "keep on asking," "keep on seeking," and "keep on knocking." Those who did would receive, find and have the door opened. If you need healing, you will be strengthened by the writings in the "Gift of Healing."

When it comes to healing, we may not know the *how* and *why* of God's ways, but we can know the how and why of what God expects from us as believers. And that is believing that He has the power to heal.

GOD STILL HEALS

I don't have to look far to find an example of God's amazing power to heal. At age thirty-five, my sister Cynthia was diagnosed with breast cancer. The surgeon found five primary sites in her left breast, which is extremely unusual. Within two weeks after the "moment of truth" that instantly changed her life, she underwent major surgery.

As the journey of cancer treatment began, she was instructed to follow a strict nutrition regimen with vitamins and a diet to help rebuild her immune system and keep her strong through treatment. It wasn't long after the surgery that the doctors informed her that they couldn't do any adjuvant therapy because there was remaining cancer that probably would not respond to treatment. She was given less than six months to live.

For months, my family and I watched her go through chemotherapy every Monday that kept her sick until Sunday, only to have to repeat the process again the following Monday. Within months she lost over fifty pounds and her hair fell out until she was completely bald. Needless to say her condition affected our entire family. Because we love her we cried when she cried, while trying to offer the spiritual and emotional support she needed. I remember my mother walking the floor in our home at night, praying that God would heal her daughter. I recall my mother holding my sister in her arms, quoting, *"by His stripes Cynthia is healed."* In spite of the doctor's report, my mother stood in faith believing that God would miraculously heal her daughter.

During one of my sister's treatments, the doctor noticed that she had begun to gain weight and build muscle. Soon afterward, the chemotherapy ceased to make her sick. Her hair began to grow back; her appetite recovered and she felt stronger. This report helped my sister to catch hold of faith, and she began to believe that there is a greater wisdom and a higher power than the doctor. Within days, my sister began to declare, "I shall live and not die."

One morning, she shared with her family, that the Lord said she was healed and would no longer need chemotherapy. As a result, she told the doctor she would no longer be taking treatments. The doctors were baffled because the lab results taken only three weeks earlier indicated that the disease was still active in her body. Shortly, however, the doctor ordered more lab tests, only to discover that from that very day, Cynthia's body was cancer-free.

My friend, I believe God can heal using doctors and nurses. I believe we should consult physicians and take full advantage of every opportunity medical science has to offer. I don't recommend abandoning medical or surgical treatments and using only prayer, because the combination of medicine and prayer can be very powerful. Unfortunately many people today misunderstand and think that if we have faith we can't use both.

In my sister's case, she believed Exodus 15:26 which says *"...for I am the LORD who heals you."* Think about that scripture for a moment. When God first revealed Himself to the people of Israel after their deliverance from Egypt, He called Himself "the Lord Who Heals." He didn't just describe Himself as a healer --He is our *healing*.

God heals because that is His pattern for revealing His nature through His Son. With compassion, Jesus chose to touch the festering sores of the leper. (Matthew 8:3.) He showed mercy as He touched the crusted lids of blinded eyes. (Matthew 9:29.) Truly our God is a healer.

In honor of Breast Cancer Awareness, I count it a privilege and a blessing to be able to share that my sister, Cynthia, has been cancer-free since 1994. To this day she remains completely free of disease. And she has been left on this earth to make a difference--and that is my prayer for you every day-that you will believe God to heal you--so that you too will be able to touch lives through your testimony of God's healing power. Cynthia spends her days sharing the gospel of Jesus Christ through song.

Give praise and thanksgiving to our wonderful God who still heals.

Scripture Reading:

Psalms 107:19-20
Then they cried to the LORD in their trouble, and he saved them from their distress. He sent forth his word and healed them; he rescued them from the grave. (NIV)

THE MIND/BODY CONNECTION

Have you ever had a headache that was stubborn and refused to go away no matter what you did to treat it? Did you ever think to examine your stressors to determine the culprit behind that persistent pain? The mind/body connection between pain symptoms and stress is well-known to scientists and medical practitioners who've been studying it for years.

In fact, wise doctors who find nothing upon diagnostic testing often probe deeper into the lives of their patients, because stress has a ripple effect that can't be denied.

Studies show that certain chronic conditions are clearly linked to emotions. Arthritis, an inflammation of the joints, can manifest due to unresolved anger, bitterness or unforgiveness. Many immune disorders and other disease processes can often be traced back to unresolved issues in victims' lives.

A friend of mine has a daughter whose husband was unfaithful, leaving her devastated and very bitter, unable to let go of her anger. Not surprisingly she ended up in the doctor's office with undiagnosed pain severe enough to keep her up walking the floors at night. After a vast array of expensive tests where they found no reason for her pain, her pastor gave her wise advice. "Because your pain is spelled a-n-g-e-r, no doctor will ever find anything wrong with you." And as she repented for her anger and gave it to God the pain began to subside and eventually disappeared entirely.

Did you know that we as human beings were never designed to carry huge emotional loads for long periods of time? When God created man He built into him adrenal glands, tiny glands located near the kidneys. Much like fuel injectors, when the need arises they shoot an adrenalin rush into the body allowing a boost of energy for a quick escape from danger. Called the *fight or flight mechanism*, it's a short term fix for an occasional problem. However, the body wasn't meant to run on such high octane fuel, because it wears out engine parts inside us in exactly the same way high octane fuel does in a race car engine.

So what are our options when these issues arise? We must examine our hearts and look for areas of unresolved emotions. If my mother rejected me as a child, I can't change her mind about that, since the only emotions I can control are my own. But I can repent of the remnant of bitterness that can so easily poison and color my world since that original incident.

Often we see ourselves as victims, wounded and scarred, and to a point there's no doubt we are, but we forget that we also have choices to make when responding to the tough situations we face.

God is there for us, and He loves us with deep compassion, but He doesn't let us off the hook when we hold onto bitterness and anger. He says the way to deal with them is to let them go, dumping them at the foot of the cross so we can be free to soar in the spirit. In fact, we can pray repeatedly for healing and see absolutely no results until we let go of the emotions that prevent such healing.

The ball is in your court now, and you have a choice to make. Will you remain a victim or let God help you put the past in the past, for the sake of your future and your health?

Ask God for His perspective on the subject, and He will show you surprising things you've never seen before. He will show you the hidden things that hinder your walk with God, the secret things you've held onto—things you didn't know existed. And then He'll gently ask for permission to clean out those corners until they're shining clean. And then He can touch and heal you.

What will your answer be?

Scripture Reading:

Psalms 22:14-15
I am poured out like water, And all My bones are out of joint; My heart is like wax; It has melted within Me. My strength is dried up like a potsherd, And My tongue clings to My jaws; You have brought Me to the dust of death. (NKJV)

THE HEALING POWER OF GOD'S LOVE

Have you ever looked at someone and thought, "Well, there's a hopeless case if I've ever seen one." Well, I'm pleased to announce that there are no hopeless cases where God is concerned. Looking at it from where we stand now we'd have to admit that we, too, were once numbered among all those other "hopeless cases."

But God made a place for us. His love makes room for even the worst offenders and, if they will accept His gift of salvation, they, too, are accepted in the beloved, and become part of the very family of God. In the process they are transformed, healed even from the most awful scars of the past, once God's love touches those places with His healing power.

Stay with me for a minute while I veer a bit further afield. Did you know that the names of women were never recorded in typical Old Testament genealogical records? Never in history were females listed, that is until the Scripture passage in Matthew 1:1-17 where five women's names are listed. Ruth, Mary, the mother of Jesus, Rahab, Tamar and Bathsheba, (Solomon's mother) who is identified only by this phrase: "by her who had been the wife of Uriah." Interestingly enough these women all have one thing in common. They were outcasts, victims and/or sinners with hopeless situations or bad reputations. Yet in the end, each of these dear women was chosen to be part of the very lineage of Jesus.

Ruth was a poverty-stricken widow and a foreigner (an outcast) from another culture, who grew to love the God of Israel. Tamar was the daughter of King David and a victim of rape who, as far as we know, never really recovered. Rahab (the mother of Boaz, and husband of Ruth) (See Joshua 2,) was a prostitute who chose to protect the lives of the two spies sent by Joshua to search out and destroy the city of Jericho. Bathsheba was seduced by King David after he killed her husband, Uriah, who'd been a captain in his army. And Mary was a low-income woman, engaged to a man, who turned up pregnant before marriage, and who never lived down her humiliation even though she bore a child who was the living embodiment of God Himself. Each of these women's lives was transformed as she submitted to God and allowed Him to work His will in her life. In the same way miracles happen when we allow God in to redeem what was lost.

It should give us all great hope to realize that though none of us deserves it God loves us with tender affection and turns things around so that we can be mightily used of Him.

And in the process, the terrible scars of our past are restored to baby fresh skin, so that all that's left is a life message that no longer haunts us, but can still affect someone's eternity.

Scripture Reading:

Psalms 19:7
The law of the Lord is perfect, converting the soul; The testimony of the Lord is sure, making wise the simple.

Part Eight: Gift of Leadership...

...is to think of your position as an opportunity to serve, not as a trumpet call to self-importance. The gift of leadership is to always hold to the principle that "people are more than things."

Leadership is not a position, but a job. It's hard and exciting and good work. One examines leadership beginning, not with techniques but rather with premise, not with tools but with beliefs, and not with systems but with understanding. This I truly believe.

Jesus was a perfect leader. He operated from a base of fixed principles or truths rather than making up the rules as he went along. Thus, his leadership style was not only correct, but also constant. Jesus said several times, "Come, follow me." His was a program of "do what I do," rather than "do what I say." I pray you will lead in this same way with others.

Not Sure Which Is Worse

Not sure which is worse? Working for your supervisor at work or working for a leader in the church. In both instances, the leader is supposed to invest in the success of his subordinates and help bring out their best qualities. But a godly leader is also required to be subject to God and his Word. Why? God requires more from a leader He's called to lead His people.

Perhaps you know those who initially loved God and walked humbly with Him, who became arrogant and disobedient, drunk on power once they were in leadership. With all my heart I believe that these men and women who began well, but finished poorly, were truly men and women of God at one point in their lives. They loved God and sought His face with a desire to please Him. But over time something happened to them just as it happened to King Saul in the Bible.

The great tragedy in Saul's life was that the power and authority of his office simply went to his head. His arrogance produced insecurity, jealousy, envy and a host of other character flaws that ultimately resulted in his fall from leadership. Although God had appointed him king, He eventually said, "I am grieved that I have made Saul king, because he has turned away from me and has not carried out my instructions" (1 Samuel 15:11 NIV).

Saul was originally made king because of the humility of his heart, but was rejected as God's choice for leadership in Israel because of his pride. Psalms 10:2 confirms that when pride enters the heart shame follows. Pride is an ugly character flaw.

Pride is nothing more than arrogance—presumption on God's grace, and cynical insensitivity toward the needs of others. Pride is both a disposition and attitude--a type of conduct that should not exist in the life of a Christian. There is pride of the eyes (Psalms 101:5); pride of the heart (Ezekiel 28:2); pride of the spirit (Proverbs 16:18); and pride of one's lips/speech. (I Samuel 2:3.)

Because of pride, Naaman refused to wash in the Jordan River (2 Kings 5:11-13), and Hezekiah displayed his wealth before the poor (Isaiah 39:2). When Uzziah grew powerful, his heart was so proud that he acted corruptly and disobeyed God. (2 Chronicles 26:16.) When Haman saw that Mordecai neither bowed down nor paid homage to him, he was filled with rage. (Esther 3:5.) The heart of the King of Tyre was so lifted up in pride that he actually claimed he *was* God. (Ezekiel 28:2.)

If you are leader in the church, don't shift ultimate confidence from God to yourself. Do not mistreat, misuse or abuse your power or disobey God's instructions. God opposes the proud. Pride will cause God to dethrone you from your area of leadership. Humble yourself under the mighty hand of God because the kingdom of God does not rise or fall on your leadership. When Saul started to think that the kingdom of God was dependent upon him, God was already working behind the scenes raising up a new leader… a humble, little shepherd boy named David to replace the proud King Saul.

If you are a leader who has to run anything, don't lead with arrogance like Saul. Humble yourself. Inspire others to take the right action and do their best. Use the Word of God as a guide and motivate your team to achieve extraordinary levels of service in God. Bottom line: the experience of working with a godly leader should always exceed the experience of working with a leader who does not know God.

Scripture Reading:

Jeremiah 23:1-2
"Woe to the shepherds who destroy and scatter the sheep of My pasture!" says the Lord. 2 Therefore thus says the Lord God of Israel against the shepherds who feed My people: "You have scattered My flock, driven them away, and not attended to them. Behold, I will attend to you for the evil of your doings," says the Lord.

There's A Lesson To Learn From Simon

Speaking of the value of honesty, I have to admit I like Simon, one of the three judges on the Fox television show, "American Idol." Although I disagree with some of his comments, I find his feedback to be extremely honest. In case you haven't seen the show, Simon's words have an ego-wounding potential. In fact, his blunt remarks make most contestants wish he would be expelled from the show. Some contestants rise to the challenges he pitches at them. Some don't. But I like Simon, because he always gives an honest answer.

Wouldn't it be nice if Christians would aim at giving honest answers? Proverbs 24:26 says: "An honest answer is like a kiss on the lips." As Christians we should always aim at giving wise answers. That is, give your opinion truthfully and everyone shall kiss your lips meaning that they will love, honor and respect you. They may not like you, but they will sincerely respect your forthright conversation.

Although it looks effortless for Simon, it's hard to tell others, especially Christians, that they need to practice more or study a little harder, at least in this venue. But think about it for a moment. The people who influenced you the most in your life were those who were your toughest critics and told you the truth. At the time they may have wounded your pride and bruised your ego, but their feedback ultimately made you better at what you do.

For example, I preached my first sermon in 1983. My scripture was taken from the book of Revelation and my subject was "God Would Rather You Be Hot or Cold, Not Lukewarm." As I approached the pulpit, I put on a deeply-sanctified look, along with the "trying-to-act-anointed-face" and preached my sermon. When service ended that night, so many Christians came to me one after another and said "I enjoyed you. You really did preach. That message was awesome." Except for one, who was an elderly church mother who sat on the front pew that evening. She said, "Baby, don't you ever preach out of the book of Revelations again until you understand it. And please don't get back in God's pulpit until you mean business for the King." My ego was devastated and crushed. And my feelings were deeply hurt, but I have never forgotten her wise words. In the end they made me think long and hard about ministry and God's call on my life.

Stop sugar coating your responses to other Christians and tell them the truth. Too many Christians in the church have American Idol Syndrome. Like Idol contestants auditioning with little or no singing ability, these people believe they are good at what they do. The Scripture tells us to encourage one another, but there is no scripture in the Bible that tells us to be dishonest with our sisters and brothers. Romans 12:17 reminds us to provide things honest in the sight of all men.

An anonymous author wrote, " If Christians were entirely honest every time they sang a hymn or gospel song, here's how some of the old favorites might sound:

- "I Surrender Some"
- "It is My Secret What God Can Do"
- "Where He Leads Me, I Might Follow" "
- "Just as I Pretend to Be"

Determine ahead of time to always to give an honest but gentle answer-- "for all liars, shall have their part in the lake which burneth with fire and brimstone: which is the second death" (Revelation 21:8).

The next time a person with no singing ability, asks how he sounded don't respond by saying, "You were awesome. You were good. You should record a CD." Just be honest and say, "You made a joyful noise unto the Lord today."

Scripture Reading:

John 8:32
And you shall know the truth, and the truth shall make you free. (NKJV)

Who, Me—Lead?

Has God called you into leadership? Perhaps you know He has, and yet your past looms over you like a giant black cloud.

Perhaps you're like a friend of mine, whose mother, wanting to protect her, subtly gave her daughter the impression that she had no gifts God could use. Over and over the mother said after the little girl's attempt at singing or reading poetry or speaking in church, "Well, that's clearly not your gift. We'll just have to keep looking." But by the time they had run through the list, no gifts remained, and the girl's self-image was shattered. Now her mother hadn't meant any harm, but it made the girl fearful to try anything. As a result she became timid, and worked in the background rather than ever stepping out into the limelight for fear of failure.

Then her mother died, and the girl heard God say that those old messages were merely her mother's opinions, not His. And He began to infuse her with courage to try new things. To her amazement she was able to master every one of them to the glory of God, who can do amazing things if we let Him.

Is fear hindering you from becoming all God wants you to be? Whose opinions have you been listening to? Do you know that esteeming someone's opinions over God's vision is actually a form of idolatry? It's true. We dare not let anything stop us from doing the will of God. In fact, we will be judged for what we did with our talents.

Consider the story of Esther, a poor orphan girl raised by her uncle. During a time of great crisis for Israel God used this simple young girl to actually save the nation. Scripture says she was born for "such a time as this." (Esther 4:14)

What about you? Were you born for such a time as this?

Scripture Reading:

Isaiah 41:9-10
I took you from the ends of the earth, from its farthest corners I called you. I said, 'You are my servant'; I have chosen you and have not rejected you. So do not fear, for I am with you; do not be dismayed, for I am your God. I will strengthen you and help you; I will uphold you with my righteous right hand. (NIV)

Part Nine: Gift of Love

Getting along with some people can be tough. How can we manage a passionate love for God and for other people? What does authentic love look like in the church, in our families, in the work place? How can we mend relationships with people who have hurt us (or people we have hurt? The answer is God's love.

God doesn't just love; He is love. His nature and essence are love. And He loves you more than anyone on this planet ever has or ever will.

There is nothing more precious than the gift of His love. And nothing can touch us more profoundly than the experience of His loving heart.

Be Kind!

We all have times when we run across those who rub us the wrong way-- those who irritate and annoy us. Does it seem like they keep popping up in your life—at home, at school, at work, in the grocery store or the shopping mall? It has become so extreme that people actually sit next to those they annoy the most just to get a rise out of them. So how do you handle it? You respond with kind words.

For months, I avoided phone calls from a particular individual, who was unkind and inconsiderate. Finally, I decided not to avoid another phone call. I watched the caller ID on my phone, patiently waiting for another call. When I finally got the call I picked up the phone and with joy in my tone, began to pray softly:

"Dear Lord, I give you praise because my friend loves you and me so much. Thank you for keeping me on my friend's mind. I am grateful that my friend feels comfortable calling me all the time. Thank you for using my friend to make me feel special and important. And because of that loving bond, I ask that you bless my friend in a special way today. Give my friend abundance and wisdom. Allow miracles to flow in my friend's life. Encourage my friend, protect my friend, and help my friend. Meet every..."

Guess what? Before I could end the prayer, the caller hung up the phone. To date, there has never been another call. In the end I concluded that God allowed this trial so I could demonstrate His love in the company of my enemy.

Nothing pleases God more than for His children to love and get along with each other. It is His desire that we dwell together in unity. A number of New Testament passages instruct us on the importance of getting along with people, both with our neighbors and with our church brethren. "Let us therefore follow after the things which make for peace, and things wherewith one may edify another" (Romans 14:19). Rather than arguing with others, we are told: "Let your [gentleness] be known unto all men . . . ." (Philippians 4:5). "Finally, be ye all of one mind, having compassion one of another, love as brethren, be pitiful, be courteous: Not rendering evil for evil, or railing for railing: but contrariwise blessing; knowing that ye are thereunto called, that ye should inherit a blessing" (1 Peter 3:8-9).

How much happiness does one experience while bickering and arguing? Not much. Many insist in getting in the "last word." Somehow the one who gets in the last word feels that he or she is the winner. The winner, however, is the one who avoids an argument in the first place. Consider this text: "Behold, how good and how pleasant it is for brethren to dwell together in unity!" (Psalms 133:1).

Start taking time to think well of and to speak well of those very people who have mistreated you. When you're tempted to feel offended, irritated or rude, choose to offer kindness instead, and see if you don't feel a new sense of peace within yourself and with your enemies.

When emotions are beginning to run high, the first question you need to ask is: How important is it? As parents we have witnessed our children squabbling over some minor thing that generally is soon forgotten. At the time that they are arguing, this becomes the most important thing in their lives. But how important is it, really? The same thing can be said about arguments that many adults have. Often couples squabble over issues they later cannot even remember. Emotions take over reasoning, and the proper perspective and importance of the issue is completely lost. Both parties generally think they are right, yet the Bible says: "There is a way which seemeth right unto a man, but the end thereof are the ways of death" (Proverbs14:12).

So the first thing to consider when any issue arises is: How important is it? If one can accurately evaluate that, he will be on the road to achieving peace-a goal the Bible says is a tremendous blessing for all involved.

My friend, be kind. Ephesians 4:32 says, "Be kind to one another, tenderhearted, forgiving each other, just as God in Christ also has forgiven you." Remember, a gentle answer turns away wrath, but a harsh word stirs up anger" (Proverbs 15:1).

Scripture Reading:

Ephesians 4:32
And be ye kind one to another, tenderhearted, forgiving one another, even as God for Christ's sake hath forgiven you.

Value Being Whose You Are

When was the last time you acknowledged and appreciated yourself? That's right--*you*. Not your spouse, not your children, not your boss, co-workers or friends. Seriously, think about it.

And if it's been a long time since you last gave yourself a pat on the back, I want you to spend the next thirty days acknowledging and appreciating yourself for everything you've accomplished. Ask yourself: How many times have I succeeded in the past month? The past year? The past ten years? Are you able to recall your successes as easily as your failures and missteps?

This is not a selfish or an egotistical act in the least. By taking the time to stop and appreciate who you are and what you've achieved--as well as what you've learned through mistakes and losses, you can actually enhance your future.

My personal experiences have taught me, that the secret of success comes with regularly acknowledging and appreciating what I have accomplished and where I've made progress.

Many Christians under-value the minor things they do successfully every day. And yet they can recall in detail every tiny mistake and failure. I want to encourage you to learn from your mistakes, but refuse to dwell on them or let them haunt you. Be gentle regarding your faults. While they once served a purpose, you are now finding new and positive behaviors to replace those old coping mechanisms. Using that attitude, you can lovingly release the old, negative patterns and habits.

Far too often, we compare ourselves to other believers and come up short. But God created you a one of a kind individual, with DNA, fingerprints and voiceprints unlike anyone else in the world. He made you that way because He wants you to know how much you matter to Him. You are unique in design and purpose, so let go of comparisons and begin to ask God what He wants to accomplish through you.

Learn to see yourself the way God sees you and love who you were meant to be, according to God's grand design. As you grow confident in your identity in Christ you will have a greater ability to love those around you, even the most unlovable.

In the days ahead learn to see yourself as a branch attached to the Vine, through whom the life of Christ is flowing. Then meditate on this scripture: Psalms 139:14--"I will give thanks to Thee, for I am fearfully and wonderfully made."

Scripture Reading:

Matthew 6:26
Look at the birds of the air; they do not sow or reap or store away in barns, and yet your heavenly Father feeds them. Are you not much more valuable than they? (NIV)

JESUS LOVES YOU

God's love defies explanation, doesn't it? At every turn mankind refused God's loving advances and rebelled against His authority, and yet He refused to give up hope. He sees us as His beloved creation, and cherishes us in a way only a father can.

He sees in us potential we can't even imagine, and holds out hope that we will finally grasp the depth of His love and come to Him.

The interesting thing is that most unbeliever and even some believers don't feel loved. Why is that? Because we know where we've been and we believe we're worthless, too far gone for God to love. And yet nothing can be further from the truth. At any time Jesus is ready and willing to run and snatch us out of the grasp of our flesh and radically transform us by the power of the blood of Christ.

God says He came as our Great Physician, because we needed healing. He already knows we're in bad shape before we know Him. It's only in relationship that transformation can take place.

So why do we wait so long, out in the cold, alone and anxious without Him? Because we can't believe that He could love us the way we are.

This is what Scripture says in Roman's 5:8—"But God commendeth His love toward us, in that while we were yet sinners, Christ died for us." Think of it this way. Sin put you in prison. Sin locked you behind the bars of guilt and shame and deception and fear. Sin did nothing but shackle you to the wall of misery. Then Christ came and paid your bail. What a gift. He served your time, satisfied the penalty and set you free.

Jesus Christ loves you.

It still blows my mind that the One who has the power to speak worlds and planets into existence and uphold them by the word of His power delights in loving His children. I am totally impressed by His commitment to be personally involved with the creatures He created.

Come to Him, fall into His arms—He's waiting to receive you.

Scripture Reading:

Isaiah 49:15
Can a woman forget her nursing child, And not have compassion on the son of her womb? Surely they may forget, Yet I will not forget you. (NKJV)

Psalms 5:7
*Because of your unfailing **love**, I can enter your house; with deepest awe I will worship at your Temple. (NLT)*

The Ten Commandments, Not the Ten Suggestions

God's laws are an expression of His love for us. Keeping those laws is an expression of our love for Him. Jesus said in John 14:15, "If you love me, you will obey what I command." I love this scripture. But even more than that, I love the basic laws of love that God gave us in the Ten Commandments. Note that they are not called "The Ten Suggestions."

In the **First Commandment** God says, "You shall have no other gods before me." This commandment teaches that love is loyal. If you told your wife, "I love you, but you also love three or four other women just as much," that's not true love, is it? True love is loyal to the object of that love.

The **Second Commandment** is "You shall not misuse the name of the LORD your God." This commandment teaches us that love is respectful. If you truly love the Lord, you will not use His name in vain or laugh when it is mocked or denigrated on TV or in someone's conversation. Of course not, because to do so would be to show disrespect not only to the name, but also to the One that name represents.

The **Third Commandment** is "Remember the Sabbath day by keeping it holy." This commandment teaches us that love is worshipful. If you truly love the Lord, are you going to take the one day you are supposed to worship Him and use it to sleep in or go to the mall or hit the golf course? Of course not! Instead, you purpose to be in His house so that you can offer to Him the praise, honor and worship He so rightly deserves.

The **Fourth Commandment** is "Honor your father and your mother." This commandment teaches quite obviously that love is honoring. It shows respect and obedience to those whom God has placed in authority over us: parents, teachers, employers, police officers, those in government. By honoring them, we are honoring God and showing our love for Him.

The **Fifth Commandment** is "You shall not murder." This commandment teaches that love is humane. If you love someone, would you try to harm or express hatred toward them? Of course not! Instead, the words of the Apostle Paul in Ephesians 4:31-32 will become your guide. There Paul says: "Get rid of all bitterness, rage and anger, brawling and slander, along with every form of malice. Be kind and compassionate to one another, forgiving each other, just as in Christ God forgave you."

The **Sixth Commandment** is "You shall not commit adultery." This commandment teaches that love is pure. If you love someone, will you seek to defile them by trying to get them into your bed outside of marriage? If you love your spouse, are you going to take that love and give it to another? Of course not! The kind of love I'm talking about here is a committed love that shows its commitment by honoring the beloved and placing their needs and desires ahead of your own.

The **Seventh Commandment** is "You shall not steal." This commandment teaches that love is considerate. If you love someone, are you going to take what they have? And if you love God, are you going to express dissatisfaction and a lack of trust in His provision by pilfering from others what God has chosen to not give you?

The Eighth Commandment is "You shall not give false testimony against your neighbor." This commandment teaches that love is truthful. If you love someone, you aren't going to tell lies about them and gossip about them, thus damaging their reputations. Nor are you going to lie to them as a way of gaining some sort of advantage over them.

Then the **Ninth and Tenth Commandments** can be summed up as "You shall not covet." These commandments teach that love is contented. Again, if you love someone, you're not going to covet what they have or become jealous or envious because they have it and you don't."

Love then is at the heart of all God's commandments. His love for us is plainly evident in them and our love for Him should be reflected in the way we keep His commandments. Romans 13:10 says: Love does no harm to its neighbor. Therefore love is the fulfillment of the law."

From now on, keep the Ten Commandments in mind when loving our neighbors. I pray, "That you may understand how wide, how long, how high, and how deep his love really Isaiah May you experience it, though it is so great you will never fully understand it" (Ephesians 3:18-19).

Scripture Reading:

Deuteronomy 28:1
Now it shall come to pass, if you diligently obey the voice of the Lord your God, to observe carefully all His commandments which I command you today, that the Lord your God will set you high above all nations of the earth.

THANK YOU

Every so often my sons and I reflect on the lost art of saying thank you, not just in children but in adults. It makes us want to examine our own lives to see how often and how well we express gratitude. What's scary is not so much that we don't say the words, but because not doing so reveals an ungrateful heart, one with an entitlement mentality. (I'm owed this.)

With that as a context, I was startled to learn that when Jesus fed the 4,000, "He took the bread, broke it, gave thanks, and distributed it." And then it says, (and this is the part I'd never seen before), "Likewise, he took the fish and gave thanks again and distributed them" (Mark 8:6-7). Isn't that amazing? Jesus gave thanks twice for the same meal.

When we give thanks, we express humility. We acknowledge that we are dependent creatures. We have no life, no hope, no health, no grace, no strength, no peace, no holiness, and nothing else that is good, apart from Christ. So we express humility. "Lord, I need you, and that's why I'm thanking you."

Being thankful means making a conscious choice to live a life that is God-centered rather than self-centered. If I'm thankful I'm not going to focus on me, my wants, my desires, or my needs. I'm going to live a life that is centered on glorifying God.

When we give thanks we exalt God. We glorify God. When we do that we fulfill the purpose for which we were created. That's why we exist--to put a spotlight on God, to glorify Him. That's what happens when we give thanks.

Psalm 50:22 tells us that there are basically two kinds of people. I want to ask you today, "Which kind of person are you?" Verse 22 says: "Consider this, you who forget God, or I will tear you to pieces, with none to rescue." That's one kind of person. It's the person who forgets God and His redemptive work on their behalf. That person, according to this verse, may be left to fend for himself in the next battle.

Verse 23 tells us about the other kind of person, "He who sacrifices thank offerings honors me" (NIV). Clearly if you're not a thankful person, then you're a person who is forgetting God. "He who sacrifices thank offerings honors me, and he prepares the way so that I may show him the salvation of God."

Those who remember to thank God for His deliverance can expect to see God act again and again on their behalf. On that note, this is my prayer for us all:

Father, thank You for this special day, a day to remember Your goodness to us. How thankful we are for Your tender mercies, Your sympathy toward us when we need You most. You watch over us through day and night. You protect us from harm's way, wrapping Your arms about us so we do not fall. Thank you for protecting us. You have kept us from danger and disaster so many times.

Thank You, Lord, for being our Shepherd. We feel confident and unafraid as You direct us each day. How blessed we are to have you as our Savior. You are unchanging. You are remarkable, extraordinary, fascinating, exciting, yet the most accessible Being in the universe.

At time, we don't have the faintest idea what is best for us, so what a relief that there is a Master Mind who does--a God with a heart full of love and with the ability to communicate with us. You lay out our future before us. Not only do You give us all we need, but You also give us things we desire.

I want to thank You for the roof over our heads, and more than enough food to eat. I want to thank You for the relationships You have given to us--for family and friends.

Thank You for all the ways You've blessed our lives and for Your loving care--for Your plan of salvation and for Your Holy Word. Thank You for our freedom and the multitude of churches where we can go to praise and worship You without fear. Thank You for every miracle, every blessing and for every open door. Thank you for the splendor of Your creation, for the beauty of this world, for the wonder of life. Thank You for the disappointments and failures that lead us to acknowledge our dependence on You. Above all, thank You for Your Son Jesus Christ; for the truth of His Word and the example of His life. Give us truly grateful hearts for Your mercies each day. Also, help us to express it to You and to others who bless us. In Jesus' name, Amen!

Scripture Reading:

1 Thessalonians 5:18
In everything give thanks; for this is the will of God in Christ Jesus for you.

Part Ten: Gift of Peace

Peace seems more difficult to find in life today and the thing most desired by us all.

The gift of peace is a mysterious gift because it is given not in the absence of anxiety but in the midst of it.

Peace has nothing to do with the situation on the outside. Peace has everything to do with the condition on the inside.

Peace is not a feeling, nor is it the absence of conflict, it is the restoration of relationship.

Jesus carefully distinguished His peace from the peace the world offers. He said, "Peace I leave with you; my peace I give you. I do not give to you as the world gives." (John 14:27)

This is the peace Paul was talking about when he wrote these words to the people of Philippi: "Do not be anxious about anything, but in everything, by prayer and petition, with thanksgiving, present your requests to God. And the peace of God, which transcends all understanding, will guard your hearts and your minds in Christ Jesus" (Philippians 4:6-7).

Are You A Peace-Breaker, Peace-Faker or Peace-Maker?

I think I understand now what Charles Dickens meant when he wrote, "It was the best of times. It was the worst of times."

There are times when life seems to move so quickly that I struggle to keep up. At times the landscape of circumstances is shaped by careful planning, investing and decisions that lead to a positive end. Then there are times when the outcome is more akin to a landslide of chaos I couldn't foresee.

Amid the uproar of a life swept away in a raging current my heart has been desperate to be alone with God. It's in this place that the litter of my overwhelmed mind is momentarily suspended, where God breaks in and let's His peace seep into my soul.

As I rest in the secret and peaceful place of the most High, I ponder the notion that Christ went to great lengths to make peace with us. It didn't matter what we looked like, how much sin we had committed, what kind of job we had or whether we were black or white. Christ made peace with us through His death on the cross.

Have you ever gone to great lengths to make peace with someone? Peace is a harmonious state of mind in which conflict is either absent or resolved without violence and in which relationships are mutually empowering and cooperative.

These days I often find myself repeating that urgent message of reconciliation to others. It's time to make peace between you and God, and then between you and man. Regardless of what others may have done to you in your past, you must love peace and work for peace in that relationship.

Think about your actions! Are you a peace-breaker, peace-faker or peace-maker?

Peace-breakers are those who go out of their way to break down relationships--to cause trouble and division. They are deliberately confrontational people who love strife and tend to disagree with everything.

Peace-fakers prefer 'peace' over truth. They will go to any lengths to avoid conflict, confrontation or unrest. In this way, they settle for a counterfeit peace based on the avoidance of real issues.

A **peace-maker** longs for peace, works for peace, and sacrifices for peace. A peace-maker does not have to constantly offer an opinion but is able to walk away quietly and avoid a conflict when the situation calls for it. Peace-makers are prepared to put others' well-being above their own comfort level. They are different from peace-fakers, because they are prepared to tell the truth and trust God for the outcome. Peace-makers are also motivated out of love--God's love.

When Jesus says, "Blessed are the peacemakers, for they shall be called the sons of God," He does not tell us how to become a son of God. He simply says that sons of God are in fact peacemakers.

God is a peace-loving and a peace-making God. Therefore, if at all possible, our goal should be to make peace with others. And while there are things we dare not trivialize or ignore, even these can be addressed with respect for the other person.

Reconciliation with others begins with God. (Genesis 32:1-2.) When we seek to enter His presence, He will reveal areas where relationships need mending and prompt us to make them right. Biblical reconciliation is powerful and spiritually rewarding. It is the process of two previously alienated parties coming to peace with one another, no longer holding onto the offenses they once had.

I charge you today, to make [follow] peace with man. (Hebrews 12:14.) As God has forgiven you, you are to forgive those who have hurt you. As God has reconciled with you, you are to reconcile with others. When you do, "May the Lord bless thee, and keep thee: The Lord make his face shine upon thee, and be gracious unto thee: The Lord lift up his countenance upon thee, and give thee peace" (Numbers 6:24-26).

Scripture Reading:

Psalms 34:14
*Depart from evil and do good; Seek **peace** and pursue it. (NKJV)*

Isaiah 32:17
*And this righteousness will bring **peace**. Quietness and confidence will fill the land forever. (NLT)*

THE ONLY PLACE TO FIND PEACE

Because we all suffer from stress, overwork and constant pressure, running at break-neck speed we often go to great lengths to find places where we can lose ourselves and find a measure of relief. These distractions may include Caribbean cruises, gambling casinos, concerts, parties, travel, movies, books, video games, shopping, and music, just to name a few. Some look for relief at the bottom of a bottle of pills or alcohol, or seek counseling to handle it. At times we spend massive sums of money in our search for the answer to the age-old question of peace. The only trouble is, once we get home we have to pay the bill, so in the end that short-term respite did little to bring us long-term peace. To say nothing of the fact, that when the vacation ends we have to return to the rat race.

So what's the answer? Where can we find peace? Isaiah 26:4 says: "Thou wilt keep him in perfect peace, whose mind is stayed on thee, because he trusteth in thee. "If that seems somewhat nebulous, let's nail it down a little further. The perfect peace of God is only found in the person of Jesus Christ and in His presence. So, rather than searching high and low only to waste time and money on futile answers for a spiritual problem, we need to go to God.

Recently I heard someone talk about "soaking" in the presence of the Lord. I had never heard that term before and was curious so I looked it up online, and found that it is a rather new term. It actually means curling up on the floor with a blanket and pillow, with worship music playing softly in the background. In that frame of mind the "soaker" basks in the presence of God, letting all distractions go and focusing on God alone. And guess what? It's the perfect place to find peace.

Several things happen in that secret place of God: First and foremost we discover that God is as close as we allow Him to be, and that He's waiting, inclining His ear to hear our cries. We're that important to Him. Secondly, we gain new perspective when we get into His presence. We can't help but step back from the urgent to find that God isn't the least bit affected by what drives us crazy.

The other place to find peace is the Word of God. He says that if we lack wisdom we only have to ask and God will answer. The intriguing thing about the Word is that God is totally on top of what we need before we even ask. And if we ask for Scriptures to meet us right where we are, He gives them without fail. Those "perfect-for-the-moment" answers are called "rhema words" and they address the questions uppermost in our minds in ways we would never imagine. And not only that, but He expands on those passages by often giving us words of knowledge if we're open to them. If you've ever sought answers in the secret place or in the Word, you know exactly what I mean. For instance, you've probably opened your Bible with no idea what scripture you needed, and when you looked down, the answer was right there in front of you.

That's the kind of God we serve. Incredible, isn't it?

Scripture Reading

Psalms 119:165
Those who love your law have great peace and do not stumble. (NLT)

THE SWEET SLEEP OF PEACE

Do you ever have trouble sleeping because of your restless mind? It's a common problem. In fact there are countless sleep aids and medications designed just for the purpose of putting us to sleep.

Often fear and dread keep us awake, worrying about this thing or that thing, though there's usually little we can do to alleviate the problem. Sometimes we have so much to do that our minds continually review our to-do list, worried that we'll forget something and be in trouble. At times we have no idea what the problem is, but for some reason sleep eludes us.

Well, sleeplessness could've been a problem for Peter in Acts 12, because he knew there was a very good chance Herod would hand down a death sentence the following morning. Peter was in jail, chained between two guards, probably on a very hard stone bench. Those things alone could have made it impossible to sleep. But let's look at what happened next. Verse 7 says: "And behold, an angel of the Lord suddenly appeared and a light shone in the cell, and he struck Peter's side and roused him, saying, 'Get up quickly.' And his chains fell off his hands." The angel told him to dress quickly and follow him out of the prison, but Peter was still so out of it that he wasn't sure if the scene was real or a dream. I find it fascinating that the angel had to hit Peter to wake him. Think about it. Would you or I have been so sound asleep in that precarious situation? I have my doubts.

How could Peter have possibly been at peace when his life was clearly in danger? Well, first of all, he was convinced that no matter what happened, either in life or in death, God would get the glory. He was persuaded that there was nothing to worry about because no matter where he went, God had already been there anticipating what would happen next.

God is still in the same business today. Scripture says He goes before us, and stands behind us, as our rear guard and our fortress. He is the shade on our right hand, and our Protection. Did you grasp that? He's not just our protector, but our very *Protection*. He covers us with His wings and unless it is our time to go, nothing will be able to harm us. And just like Peter we can be secure in the love of our wonderful God, and sleep like babies.

Scripture Reading

Isaiah 26:3
You will keep him in perfect peace, Whose mind is stayed on You, Because he trusts in You. (NKJ)

Part Eleven: Gift of Prayer

We today yearn for prayer and hide from prayer. We are attracted to it and repelled by it. We believe prayer is something we should do, but are guilty of not praying as often as we should.

We are not sure of what holds us back. Of course we are busy with life, but that is only a smoke screen because we somehow find time for all other obligations.

God's Word tells us to pray. But we don't pray just because we have to; we pray because talking to God is a privilege.

Prayer was the priority in Jesus' life. It was the primary communication link between Himself and the Father. If we are to be Christ-like, or like Christ, we must follow His example and pray.

The Incredible Power of Prayer

I frequently receive e-mails from believers world-wide who share how the enemy is trying to overwhelm and destroy them under the terrible pressures of life. Many face terminal illnesses and need a mighty move of God. Some are at the end of their strength, weary of the battle and ready to give up. Others feel hopeless and struggle even to keep going. The battle is very real.

Some send cries for help via letter, sharing desperate financial situations, relationship problems, and job losses among other things. Some need spiritual direction, regarding their purpose and destiny. And while their problems can sometimes seem overwhelming these are our brothers and sisters in Christ, and they need our prayer support.

Scripture says that prayer changes things. In fact, it sets heaven in motion when you and I dare to pray. And by faith we must believe that we can impact an immeasurable amount of suffering by our prayers. By praying you can participate in redeeming a soul, strengthening a weary heart, and encouraging the brokenhearted. Scripture says our prayers are powerful to the breaking down of strongholds.

No words can express the power we have when we touch and agree in Jesus' name. I am a firm believer that there is no limit to God's power, especially where two or more join forces. God Himself said, "Behold, I am Jehovah, the God of all flesh. Is there anything too hard for me?" (Jer. 32:27). The answer is no. Our God is not weak, nor incapable, nor without power to heal the soul and meet every need. God's power can overcome the work of the enemy every time, but only if we pray.

So let's Pray...........

Father God, in the Name of Jesus:

I stand in agreement with my friends as we lift up your children who are in desperate need of Your touch, intervention, guidance, strength and healing.

Lord, some of your children have been in a struggle so long, that their spirit is saying "Lord, how much longer?" The battle has been so great that it has stolen their hope for the future and weakened their faith so they feel like giving up. We are pressed in with problems, uncertainty, and fear on every side. You promised You would never leave or forsake us. Despite how we feel, I know You are holding our hand each day, gently leading us through bad times so we may experience good times.

Thank You for Your Promise that You will shine Your glorious light upon Your children. We place our hands in Yours and look forward with great expectation that You will come through for us. Keep us anchored in Your steadfast love as we trust in You. We expect your mighty power to calm our raging seas and perform the impossible things in our lives.

God, we plead your precious blood over each one of your sons and daughters. You are abundantly more than sufficient and able to heal and help your children. Empower them to hold on and trust your Word. Give them peace in the midst of the storm and the grace to be still and know that You are God.

Now Lord, we believe Your grace is sufficient to carry us through. We believe that You are restoring order to every chaotic situation even now. For You are El Shaddai, Almighty One, God.

Thank You for the victory. Thank You for the healing. Thank You for the miracles. Thank you for answering our prayers. Thank You, dear Lord, for Your help and peace. In Jesus' name we pray, Amen!

Scripture Reading:

Genesis 24:42
*So this afternoon when I came to the spring I prayed this **prayer**: 'O LORD, the God of my master, Abraham, if you are planning to make my mission a success, please guide me in a special way. (NLT)*

Matthew 7:7
Ask and it shall be given, seek and ye shall find, knock and it shall be opened unto you.

National Day of Prayer

The National Day of Prayer was designated by the United States Congress as a day when people are asked to come together to pray. It was created as a floating holiday in 1952 and fixed on the first Thursday in May by Ronald Reagan.

In case you're unaware of it, the National Day of Prayer is currently under attack by radicals determined to silence any expression of faith. But you can help defend the National Day of Prayer by joining your brothers and sisters in prayer. No matter where you are on that day, I encourage you to pray. Pray for our country, for our representatives to rise up and be bold, declaring that right is right and wrong is wrong, declaring that America is a Christian nation founded on the truth of the gospel. Pray that the Lord would send a mighty spirit of revival that would shut the lions' mouths and turn around for good what our enemy means for harm. Pray that the glory of God will be revealed once again across our land as we take back the ground the devil has stolen away. Let the redeemed of the Lord say so, while there's still time to take a stand for righteousness!

Here is my prayer for you today:

I war for the release of finances and all resources that belong to you; that everything prepared for you before the foundation of the world, that pertains to your life (i.e., ministry, calling) shall come to you now. You will not be denied. You shall not be overlooked. You will not accept substitutes. You shall call in resources from the north, south, east and west.

I decree and declare that every resource necessary for you to fulfill God's original plans and purposes comes to you without delay.

I decree and declare that the wealth of the wicked is no longer laying up for you but is now released. Let those who have held on to your wealth longer than they should have, be miserable until they release what rightfully belongs to you. I command Satan to "cough it up," release it, spit it out, loose it and let it go now.

I decree and declare that God brings you into a wealthy place. I declare that you will increase in substance and prosper in the land where you have been strategically planted.

I decree and declare that the schemes, plots and snares of the enemy that have been targeted against your life are destroyed. You will no longer be oppressed, suppressed, restrained, hindered or blocked by others who refused to acknowledge the anointing and calling upon your life.

I pray that you are protected from diabolical, cruel, evil and satanic activities. You are covered by the blood of Jesus--protected under His wings and hidden in His secret place.

I rebuke every disturbance, annoyance and irritation that has come to disrupt and threaten your peace and tranquility. You will no longer be harassed by envious, jealous and resentful enemies. I command Satan, and your enemies to become your footstool today.

I pray that your finances, marriage, relationships, ministries, sicknesses and diseases be healed. I pray that God will open the windows of heaven and release blessings and miracles into your life.

Jehovah Jireh, loose the lions of kings! Go before your children and make the crooked places straight. Grant unto your sons and daughters, according to Your riches in glory. Let their anointing flow unhindered and uncontaminated in their lives.

Lord Jesus, allow your children to recognize that their season is in your hands and it shall not be altered or adjusted by anyone or anything.

I pray that your sons and daughters will take time to call on Your name. For when we pray and humble ourselves before You, You promised to heal our land.

Father, the issue of public prayer is increasingly controversial in an age of religious diversity and increasing secularization. So I pray for the leaders who govern and defend our land. Although our government thinks it is appropriate to remove Your Son's name from a spoken prayer, His existence cannot be removed or detached from Your creation. Jesus is real. In Him, we live, and move and have our being.

Thank You Father, for sending Your Son, Jesus to save us. We give You praise right now, before we see a single answer, because that is the faith that pleases You. In Jesus' all-powerful name, Amen!

Scripture Reading

Luke 18:1
And he spake a parable unto them to this end, that men ought always to pray, and not to faint.

A Word From the Lord Just For You

Perhaps today is a day when you wished you could stay in bed with the covers over your head until your trial or test is over. But may I remind you that I, God "know the plans I have for you" (Jeremiah 29:11).

I am always watching over you, no matter where you are or how difficult times may be for you. There is no limit to My power as I help you. Trust me and do My will. Delight in Me. Commit your will to Me. Quiet yourself before Me and wait upon My direction. Flee from fighting and anger. Never seek revenge. I will fight the battle for you.

If it appears that all of hell is against you, it is! But this is not the time to allow the whispers of the naysayers to get through to you. "Be still and know that I am your God" (Psalms 46:10). It is in My presence that you can be still. Your heart, spirit and mind must be still, if you are to recognize my voice during your time of affliction.

I have given you a glimpse of what I have in store for you. I have revealed to you things to come. I have given you much revelation of who you are, but prevented you from moving forward, for it was not yet time. You have learned much, suffered much, and have been rejected much. I allowed it, so that I can bring you forth, under My name and no other.

I know the plans I have for you, and I only used this avenue to make My plans clear to you. It is I who have asked you to walk by faith, not by feeling or sight. This is the only way that you will be able to perform the tasks ahead of you.

My child, you are about to emerge from this test. Go back to sleep. My word that you have consistently spoken shall perform for you this day. Trust me with your life. I, God am ordering your steps.

Scripture Reading:

John 16:13
But when he, the Spirit of truth, comes, he will guide you into all truth. He will not speak on his own; he will speak only what he hears, and he will tell you what is yet to come. (NIV)

Part Twelve: Gift of Seasons

What season of life are you in? Are you experiencing a winter of discouragement blowing like a cold wind through your soul? Or do you feel the exuberance of spring renewal, the lazy warmth of summer rest. Perhaps the wind of change has brought in autumn of reflection in your heart during the fall.

Exploring the relationship between the seasons of the earth and the seasons of our lives, they help us discover the seasons as stepping stones along the path of the great circle of life and guides for life's journey.

Whatever season you are in, be content. Seasons do change.

Spring: It's Not Just Another Season!

Springtime always means the earliest, freshest, and most pleasant season of all, because all things are new. Can you expect great things for yourself? Yes, indeed you can. Will you? That's completely up to you.

Motivational speaker Ralph Marston said *"All the things you hope to become, all the things you would like to accomplish, all the things you plan to do, don't carry much weight in comparison to those things you actually expect to become, to accomplish and to do."* I agree with his statement because the best-crafted plans are meaningless unless you sincerely expect to follow through on them. The most magnificent dreams will elude you until you can truly and confidently expect to achieve them and work toward that end. So why not make it happen in the springtime?

Spring is the time to be active, energetic, vigorous and full of life. Spring means to leap over something: to leap over a barrier; to emerge rapidly: to appear or come into existence quickly; to move back to an original position after being forced in another direction and to originate from a particular source. I'd like to share a few words of wisdom from these definitions to help us set our course for spring.

To spring means "to leap over something: to leap over a barrier." Never get left behind when the time is right. Leap with joy over every single barrier to your natural and spiritual success by running with the vision that God has given you. Because you must move with time, every now and then you should get in the fast lane to overtake those who are attempting to slow you down. You cannot afford to let the devil chase you this time. You must put him on the run. Leap for everything that is yours. To leap is to move aggressively, decisively and swiftly. You do not have the time to remove obstacles, problems or hindrances. It's time to leap over them. Because you do not have time to waste, jump as high as you can and keep on moving. This is your opportunity to redeem the time, so do it in the name of Jesus and start leaping over every barrier in your life.

To spring means "to emerge rapidly: to appear or come into existence quickly." Listen, if you're going to plant anything, build anything, launch out into any kind of ministry, this is the time to do it. This is the time to assertively go forth! We should be like Nehemiah. We need to know the season we are in, be focused, have a sword in one hand and a hammer in the other! Like Nehemiah, we need to be aggressive in order to go all the way. Mathew 11:12 says, "The kingdom of heaven suffers violence, and the violent take it by force." When we put our faith in action, God will show us how great He can be and what He can do rapidly.

Springtime births acceleration. Acceleration means things begin to spring forth, step up, speed up, hurry up, and come forth at an increased rate. Get ready for God to bring you before great men. (Proverbs 19:16.) Remember, the struggle is not in getting in front of great men. The struggle is in developing yourself to the point where great men want some of what you have.

To spring means "to move back to an original position after being forced in another direction." I have come to realize that having a passion for something does not necessarily mean that God is calling you to that particular thing. In fact, just the opposite may be true. Every so often, we may have departed from God's will and veered off the course to please others in the body of Christ. And if that's the case it is time to return to God. Returning to God means returning to the course God intended you to be on. We all have the freedom to do whatever we want and to live the life that we want to live (1 Corinthians 10:23). But not everything we want to do is beneficial and according to the will of God. God reminds the people, through Jeremiah that they are walking upon a path that is far from His will, and as a result their souls are weary. (Jeremiah 6:6) To find rest for their souls, they must return to God. If someone or something has forced you away from the will of God, turn back to Him so He can fulfill His plan in you. If you're not sure of your direction examine yourself and seek God's face. Self-examination seeks the truth regarding whether we are truly in the faith as well as what sins stand between us and the will of God for our lives. The Word of God says, "Let us search out and examine our ways, and turn back to the LORD" (Lamentations 3:40).

"Spring" means: "to originate from a particular source." To know your authority is to know your identity. Using my life as an example, as God began to shed light on my destiny, one of the first scriptures He directed me too was Luke 1:76–79. So I asked Him how that scripture applied to me, and He said: "That's your call: to preach the gospel, prepare the way of the Lord, and preach the gospel of repentance and the remission of sin.

I've called you not only to be light in the midst of darkness, but to bring light for those that are in darkness, and to set the captive free." Wanting to comprehend what it all meant, I asked the Lord, "Is that really who I am?" and God answered, "Not only is that who you are but if you want a real revelation of who you are then read every scripture that has the phrase 'servant of the Lord.' Study every chapter, every scripture reference to the ministry of the servant of the Lord because as the Father has sent Me, so I send you (John 20:21). It's the same call; it's the same anointing: "as the Father has sent Me, so I send you also." Therefore, out of respect for what God said I began researching every promise, and one day I had a revelation of the gospel of the kingdom; understood who I was, what God called me to, who Jesus is, and who Jesus is in me. That revelation changed my life. I could now move ahead into ministry, confident in Christ. My expectation was full of faith that God's power would truly flow through me. After all, He created my call! Guess what? He also created your call and created you for His glory.

Spring is here. It is not just another season, but a time for growth, renewal and new life. It is the start of better times--the time to "spring into action."

Scripture Reading:

Deuteronomy 2:31
And the Lord said to me, 'See, I have begun to deliver Sihon over to you. Begin to occupy so that you may possess his land.

HE MAKES EVERYTHING BEAUTIFUL IN HIS TIME

From the very beginning of time God has had a plan, a masterpiece of creation designed for us to enjoy with Him. Because He loves us, His heart's desire is for us to enjoy the fullness of His plans, personal plans that include a future and a hope custom-made just for us.

So why is it we so often settle for less? Because it's risky, scary to let go and trade what we have now for what's behind Door Number One, a mystery that has yet to be revealed.

But God isn't a man that He should lie. (See Numbers 23:19.) He left His Word here to persuade us of His good intentions for us, and yet so often we refuse to believe anyone could be that good, that kind, that beneficent. And yet He is.

He sees us with the eyes of love, weeps with us when we grieve, and wants to enter into our lives, and be intimate, comforting, encouraging, able to restore what this cantankerous world and the devil have stolen away. He wants us to see ourselves as He sees us, wants to make everything beautiful again. He really does. And it's possible as we spend time with Him, letting Him overcome the obstacles the world tosses before us to trip us up. One by one, He pushes aside those obstacles and helps us to our feet, takes our hand as we walk together, and on occasion, even carries us when we're too weary to go any farther.

It's been said that what we tell ourselves over and over becomes what we believe. So when we get into the Word and take it in, we are transformed, truly transformed by the daily renewing of our minds, so that what we used to doubt, now changes the very essence of who we are. That's why Scripture says all things become new in Christ.

Drink in the truth--that He sees you as a beautiful, one-of-a-kind individual unlike any other, and He has plans that no one but you can fulfill. And as you spend time in His presence the beauty of holiness will transform you into what He created you to be so that thing in your hand, the one you didn't want to give up, will fall with a clank to the floor, no longer worthy of mention.

Scripture Reading:

Ecclesiastics 3:11
He has made everything beautiful (appropriate) in its time. He has also set eternity in the hearts of men; yet they cannot fathom what God has done from beginning to end. (NIV)

To Everything There is a Season

Ecclesiastes 3:2-8 continues: "A time to be born, and a time to die; a time to plant, and a time to pluck up that which is planted; a time to kill and a time to heal; a time to break down, and a time to build up; a time to weep and a time to laugh; a time to mourn, and a time to dance; a time to cast away stones, and a time to gather stones together; a time to embrace and a time to refrain from embracing, a time to get, and a time to lose; a time to keep, and a time to cast away; a time to rend, and a time to sew, a time to keep silence and a time to speak; a time to love and a time to hate; a time of war and a time of peace."

So how can we know what to do? How can we know what to do next-- whether to speak or be silent? It takes wisdom to know what to do in the moment, doesn't it? So where do we get wisdom? Scripture tells us wisdom comes from God. James 1:5 says, "But if any of you lacks wisdom let him ask of God who gives to all men generously and without reproach, and it will be given to him."

Have you ever dealt with a sudden, unexpected crisis and had no idea what to do? We all have situations when we have little time to decide, yet the future hangs in the balance depending on the wisdom of the moment.

God knows the beginning from the end. He knows the result of our next move, and He's more than willing to equip us for the moment, because He wants us to succeed. But we must humble ourselves to ask for wisdom. We must let go of fear and condemnation and trust God, knowing He knows the future. Scripture also says we have not because we ask not. (James 4:2) So when God is in control, we can be assured that His wisdom holds wondrous treasures, whose value is far beyond that of silver and gold.

Draw near to God and equip yourself for every season, for He has the answers you need. He is good and His mercy endures forever.

Scripture Reading:

Ecclesiastics 3:1
To everything there is a season and a time to every purpose under heaven.

Part Thirteen: Gift of Rest

After a long day, most of us feel utterly ransacked. We are waylaid by endless demands and routines. Even our vacations have a panicky task-like edge to them. "If I only had more time," is the mantra of our age. But is this the real problem? No!

What we've really lost is the "rest of God–that part of Himself we can only know through stillness.

Rest is essential to our humanity and faith. God, knowing that, and knowing how easily we might neglect it, made it a command. We've neglected it anyhow. We've lost the rest of God.

Hopefully, the writings in this section will change that.

SOMEBODY FIND THE OFF SWITCH

You are probably dealing with stress: If you find yourself saying, "Hand over the chocolates and no one will get hurt."

What is stress? This definition is from the *Idiot's Guide To Dealing With Stress*: "Stress is what you experience when you feel you cannot cope effectively with a threatening situation." Stress is both a noun and a verb. We possess it and we react to it.

There is a difference between feeling stressed and becoming distressed. When we are distressed, the first thing to go is our ability to sleep. We go over and over and over the things that are bothering us. When we are unable to cope, that's a sign of distress, usually accompanied by feelings of helplessness, hopelessness, and despair. We feel defeated. We develop spiritual apathy, feeling like we can no longer adequately communicate with God.

When stress becomes chronic, we begin to experience an impact on our health and on our relationships.

So How Do We Deal With These Things?

Start with the Lord. The truth is, it's impossible to meet the demands of the day without Jesus. Even when time is short we can worship and praise God throughout the day. Put the worship tape on in the car and get into the presence of God, taking Him with you wherever you go.

We also need to lay at the feet of Jesus the things we cannot change. We must learn to say, "Father, I have no control over this situation. The choices that are being made are not mine. I wouldn't have chosen them. I don't want them. So I give them to You."

You can also reduce the stress in your life by organizing your day into segments so you accomplish the essentials. Find time for yourself. Take ten minutes to rest throughout your day, even if you just sit on a stool and drink a cappuccino. Exercise at least fifteen minutes three times a week and set boundaries. Associate with people who make you laugh and not make you cry. And learn to look for humor in every situation.

The sad truth is stress is not going to go away - at least not on earth. Find out what's really behind that stress. Clear the clutter, organize, find time for yourself, find people who can build you up, and laugh. Then you can more easily manage the stress in your life instead of desperately seeking the "off" switch.

Scripture Reading:

Isaiah 40:28-29
Do you not know? Have you not heard? The LORD is the everlasting God, the Creator of the ends of the earth. He will not grow tired or weary, and his understanding no one can fathom. He gives strength to the weary and increases the power of the weak. (NIV)

STOPPING TO RECHARGE

For a long time I resisted the idea of carrying a cell phone. But as much as I have to communicate from the road, my cell phone has become essential. It is battery operated, which means, it will not run indefinitely. And it is no fun to be in a situation where you really need to communicate, and you find your cell phone DOA. So every few days, I make sure to plug my cell phone into a recharger, so it is good to go again.

Just as a cell phone needs down time to recharge, so do you and I. We need to take time for adequate rest. In fact, God created us that way. Rest is one of the Sabbath principles that He built into our creation, because He did not intend for us to work all the time. In Genesis 49:15, God said that rest is a good thing.

Several years ago I found myself with way too many commitments in too few days. I was nervous and tense about it. I was impatient with people, driving to every appointment in a hurry, and feeling irritated at those unexpected but predictable interruptions that are part of every day. Before long, everything in my life started reflecting the tension of my harried coping style. It was becoming unbearable and agonizing.

One evening after supper I distinctly remember the words of my youngest son, Stedmon who wanted to share something that happened at school that day. Speaking quickly he said, "Mom, I want to tell you something, and I'll tell you really, really fast." Suddenly realizing his frustration, I answered, "Son, you can tell me--and you don't have to tell me really, really fast. Say it slowly." I will never forget his answer: "Mom, then listen slowly." His words taught me a valuable lesson I will never forget...*to slow down.*

Are you rushing headlong through the fast lane? If so you are stressed, fatigued, impatient, irritable, and addicted to the adrenaline rush. At this rate, you'll find yourself going over the edge or sending the people around you over the edge. You have to stop to recharge. Your physical and emotional batteries cannot run indefinitely without a complete breakdown of all systems.

As Christians, often times we go too fast and find ourselves spinning out of control. Next, comes the "crash and burn" phase, which we all want to avoid. However, there is a stress reduction prescription found in the Word of God. Mark 6, verse 31 says, "And he said unto them, Come ye yourselves apart into a desert place, and rest a while: for there were many coming and going and they had no leisure so much as to eat." Where can you get rest? In the desert! A quiet place where you are isolated and inaccessible, with no interruptions. A place that shifts you, in to down time.

It's the down time that recharges the battery of my cell phone. It's the down time that allows my battery to reset, revitalize and renew. It is the down time that regenerates and rejuvenates my physical, emotional and spiritual batteries. If I don't give my phone battery that recovery time, it eventually won't work at all. The same applies to recharging our bodies with rest.

Though we may believe otherwise rest is not a waste of time. Rather it's much like giving your body a mini-vacation to prepare for the next day, while it gives your brain a chance to sort things out. And much like the cell phone battery, without recovery time, eventually those systems won't work at all. Rest has the effect of recharging all systems so we can run again at full power.

As a card-carrying ex-workaholic myself I know how easy it is to fill every moment until there isn't a spare second to breathe. And while it may make us feel indispensable, its cost is enormous in emotional peace, in close relationships, and even in performance and creativity. God created in us the need to take time out to rest and restore so that in the end we actually get much more done in much less time.

You may admit that you need rest. But it won't happen unless you make a non-negotiable commitment to do it. Schedule it on your calendar. Stand back, re-examine your priorities, and literally schedule regular times to recharge. Write them on your calendar. For example, set a firm quitting time. A time when you step out of your normal routine and you do nothing but rest. You may be saying, "I am too busy to take a time-out." Well, I'm saying "You're too busy not to." Without balancing mechanisms such as rest and relaxation, you will literally burn out and be of little use to the kingdom of God.

Scripture Reading:

Isaiah 49:31
But those who hope in the LORD will renew their strength. They will soar on wings like eagles; they will run and not grow weary, they will walk and not be faint. (NIV)

No Compromise

The concept of "compromise" can have its place, but not often in the life of a Christian. It may mean cooperating when there is nothing at stake, and in that sense it's okay, but these days it's more likely to mean fighting for what's right.

In our day it takes strength to keep from backing down when we're tempted to compromise. And, in case you haven't noticed, compromise is everywhere. At work, and even at home, with our husbands and children. We see it at church, out shopping, in the voter booth, even in our hearts. And it's easy to think, *What will it hurt if I "_____"* and you fill in the blank. "Spend a little extra..." "Let Johnny run around with that new friend I haven't yet met..." "Look the other way when my co-worker cheats on his mileage and time sheets..." "See a questionable website on a Christian's computer screen..." "Vote for this man even if he's pro-abortion..." "Say nothing when I hear a harmful rumor..." "Don't speak up when my congressman votes against what's right..."

It's probably easier to count the minutes we don't see compromise, than the ones in which we do, because examples abound everywhere we look. It can be exhausting to fight on every front every day, and yet that's exactly what God calls us to do. The slippery slope is steep and we're headed that way at breathtaking speeds now. So when we become weary in well-doing it behooves us to remember that *all it takes for evil to succeed is for good men to do nothing.* (Roman Emperor Augustus.)

A few years ago a friend of mine had a daughter who, as an early teen, walked away from God. And not surprisingly my friend grew exhausted trying to hold the line for God. On occasion when she was at her wits' end she would ask, "Is it all right if I just stop arguing with her at every turn and simply be her friend?" And I would say, "Nope. It's not okay, because these are God's standards and they're not negotiable. You have to hold up the standard no matter what. If she has trouble you tell her to go argue with God, because you will not back down." And I would hold her up in prayer. And while it took years to see the fruit of our labor, the girl eventually turned her heart back to the Lord, and is serving Him today. What would've happened if my friend had simply given up the fight and let the status quo stand? Her daughter may never have returned to the Lord. That's how vital these issues are.

We were put on earth to be light and salt to a lost and dying world, so if we don't do it, who will? In fact, the reason most unbelievers don't think much of Christians and Christianity is that we have done little to demonstrate our integrity. But it's never too late to change the impression we've left in the past. That's why, no matter how weary we are we need to ask God to strengthen our resolve to do right. And when we do He will run to our aid and infuse us with courage, physical stamina, perseverance and the spiritual and emotional fortitude to get in there and stand up for what's right. We may not see immediate results, but God is keeping score, and He says our efforts are a sweet smelling fragrance, a perfume in heaven, and He is pleased.

Scripture Reading:

Matthew 5:13
"You are the salt of the earth. But if the salt loses its saltiness, how can it be made salty again? It is no longer good for anything, except to be thrown out and trampled by men. (NIV)

Part Fourteen: Gift of Wisdom

Where our own understanding fails, there is something greater to lean on–God's wisdom.

Wisdom empowers our Christian life. Wisdom gives us direction and leads us to the freedom of living a godly life.

In Proverbs it says we are to "cry aloud for understanding... look for it [wisdom] as for silver and search for it as for hidden treasure." (2:3-4)

Knowing God's wisdom in your everyday decision-making will help you overcome those issues that so often seem insurmountable through human understanding alone.

Learn to receive the power of godly wisdom.

Don't Be a Fool

God has a lot to say about fools and foolishness. In fact, some form of the word "fool" is used 189 times in the King James Version of the Bible. In our society, we have several expressions about being a fool. One of them is "I am nobody's fool." None of us wants to be considered foolish. I invite you to stop a moment to consider some of the things God says that "any fool can do."

God says any fool can start a quarrel. "It is honorable for a man to stop striving, since any fool can start a quarrel" (Proverbs 20:3 NKJV). Which takes more strength of character, walking away from an argument or starting one? It takes an honorable man to break the cycle of strife and contention. Any fool can quarrel. "A fool's mouth is his destruction, and his lips are the snare of his soul" (Proverbs 18:7). Be a person of honor, rather than a fool.

Any fool can declare himself to be right. "The way of a fool is right in his own eyes, but he who heeds counsel is wise" (Proverbs 12:15). If we are our own standard of right and wrong, God says we are fools! Wasn't this the problem the children of Israel had during the time of the Judges? "…everyone did what was right in his own eyes" (Judges 17:6). If you are wise, listen to God, not to your wayward mind. Listen to others who love you. Any fool can go through life thinking that he needs no one but himself. It takes a wise man to admit that he needs good counsel.

Any fool can get in over his head! Have you ever known someone who didn't know when to admit that he didn't know? You see, some things are just too lofty (over the head) for a fool. "Wisdom is too lofty for a fool; He does not open his mouth in the gate" (Proverbs 24:7). A fool does not grasp the greatness of our Lord. "O Lord, how great are your works! Your thoughts are very deep. A senseless man does not know, nor does a fool understand this" (Psalms 92:5, 6).

Any fool can make evil his past time. "To do evil is like sport to a fool, but a man of understanding has wisdom" (Proverbs 10:23). Is this not a sad commentary on the very society in which we live? One does not have to look very far to realize that evil has become the past time for many. Whether it be gambling, drinking, drugs, pornography, fornication or just plain selfishness, our society has very little understanding of God's ways. How sad. Be a person of understanding. Any fool can do evil.

Any fool can say that there is no God. "The fool has said in his heart, there is no God"…" (Psalms 14:1). How foolish it is to think we will escape the judgment of God. "Yet they say, the Lord does not see, nor does the God of Jacob understand. Understand you senseless among the people; And you fools, when will you be wise?" (Psalms 94:7-8). Many will face a "great awakening" but by then it will be too late. Any fool can do as they please, ignore God, and think they answer to no one but themselves.

Before we became Christian, we too were once foolish. Thanks be to God we have turned from that vain way of life. "For we ourselves were also once foolish, disobedient, deceived, serving various lusts and pleasures, living in malice and envy, hateful and hating one another. But when the kindness and the love of God our Savior toward man appeared…He saved us…" (Titus 3:3-5).

Any fool can reject Christ but if you heed His call, you will indeed be wise. "But we preach Christ crucified, to the Jews a stumbling block and to the Greeks foolishness, but to those who are called, both Jews and Greeks, Christ the power of God and the wisdom of God" (1 Corinthians 1:23-24).

Don't be a fool! Accept God's invitation, and be wise.

Scripture Reading:

Ephesians 5:17
Therefore do not be foolish, but understand what the Lord's will is. (NIV)

Have You Been Deceived Lately?

If I were to insult you, you'd feel the sting immediately. If I were to embarrass you, you'd be the first to know. But if I were to deceive you... you might never know it!

As painful as being insulted or embarrassed can be, at least you are aware of what's taking place. But deception can be deadly because you don't realize you are being betrayed, misled, seduced or ensnared. It's much more than clever sleight of hand.

Deception can take so many different forms that it is impossible to describe all the ways a person can mislead you. It's not pleasant to think about being betrayed by someone, but it does happen. And it can happen in the body of Christ.

According to Webster's Dictionary the word "deceive" means: "to lead astray or to cause to accept as true or valid what is false or invalid." I describe a "deceitful person" as someone who hides malicious intent under the guise of kindliness. Jesus describes a deceitful person as a wolf in sheep's clothing.

Jesus warned His followers in Matthew 7:15: "Beware of the false prophets, who come to you in sheep's clothing, but inwardly are ravenous wolves." That warning was important because Jesus later said to them: "Behold, I send you out as sheep in the midst of wolves; therefore be shrewd as serpents, and innocent as doves" (Matthew 10:16). The apostle Paul penned a similar warning: "I know that after my departure savage wolves will come in among you, not sparing the flock" (Acts 20:29).

Wolves are known to be merciless, ferocious and ravenous. Wolves are the most common enemies of sheep. Once upon a time a wolf resolved to disguise his appearance in order to secure food more easily. Encased in the skin of a sheep, he pastured with the flock deceiving the shepherd by his costume.

Some people are like wolves who pretend to be sheep. They act and dress like the sheep, only to destroy the lambs once they are among them. "They come to you in sheep's clothing;" that is, with an appearance of harmlessness. They come in the most mild, inoffensive manner, without any obvious evidence of enmity. As a result, you see no reason to suspect that they have even the desire to do harm. But that is not all. They come, secondly, with an appearance of usefulness. But instead, they are evil, devious, cunning, dishonest, deceptive, unreliable and misleading.

As believers, we can determine which sheep are true sheep, and which are wolves. Jesus said we'll know, because even if a wolf is dressed like a sheep, it will act like a wolf. For instance, a wolf can't bleat like a sheep; it can't chew cud like a sheep; and it can't eat grass or even smell like a sheep. The wolf can even try to look like a sheep, but you can distinguish the sheep from a wolf, by its actions.

In the same way, Satan will do whatever he can to destroy the flock (the children of God). Therefore, it is imperative that we have discerning spirits so we can discern the motives of those who are among us. For your own good, don't be quick to jump into a relationship. Don't rush to add someone to your team because they appear to be useful. Don't be quick to give someone a position in the church because they appear to be kind. I believe the greatest danger to the work of the kingdom of God is to have a team of wolves dressed as sheep leading God's people.

From now on let's pray before we link up with others, even those who claim to be Christians. Not sure who to connect with? Matthew 7:16 says, "You shall know them by their fruit."

Scripture Reading:

1 John 3:7
Little children, let no one deceive you. He who practices righteousness is righteous, just as He is righteous. (NKJV)

Terrible Two Christians

When I was pregnant with my first child, Steven, many other mothers told me about their child rearing experiences, especially the "terrible two" stage. I was told that at two years of age kids often test their parents. In fact, they're notorious for temper tantrums occurring any time and any place when they don't get their way.

My first experience with a tantrum was nineteen years ago when my son was two years old. I recall the moment as if it were yesterday. He picked up a candy bar and looked at me. When I took it from him he began to scream and kick his feet. Quietly I said, "Steven, be quiet, and be nice. But instead his screams increased with intensity. During this era, the child abuse laws were being widely televised, so when I realized how many people were watching our little drama, I caved in and handed him the candy.

I had read many books on "how-to" handle the terrible two's. But none of them seemed to work that day in the supermarket. But one day, he threw himself on the living room floor, screaming and kicking for dear life, going through his bag of tricks that had so annoyed me in the supermarket. But that time things were different, because I stood in complete silence to get his attention. When he'd ended all the drama our eyes met.

At that point, I knew one of two things would happen: 1) he would either fall asleep from fatigue or 2) he would mimic my actions and stop and look at me in silence. It was only then, with no other option that he was able to hear when I spoke in a soft voice.

Here's my point…..

Perhaps you've wanted something from God, and you asked Him for it, but he said "No," but you wanted it so bad that you refused to bow to His will. Consequently, you did everything you could do in your own power to make it happen. However, in spite of your complaining, blaming, grumbling and whining, He never said a single word. Soon you were exhausted, too weary to scream anymore. It was only then that you were able to hear His voice.

If you are at a point in your life, where the Lord seems to be silent? Maybe He's just waiting to get your attention. He has mighty things to show you and speak to you about. But how can He speak if you're act like a terrible two? Ask God to quiet your spirit, so you hear His voice. Psalm 107:30 says: "Then are they glad because they be quiet...."

Scripture Reading:

Psalms 32:9
Do not be like the horse or like the mule, Which have no understanding, Which must be harnessed with bit and bridle, Else they will not come near you.

Spiritual Boundaries—A Principle We All Need

I can guarantee that, if you have not yet drawn boundaries and all of a sudden, you break out your brand new, never-been-used-before magic marker and draw a line in the sand, people are going to get upset, wondering why you're doing it now. After all, you've never drawn a line before.

Sometimes it is hard to set boundaries with others. We all want to be liked and to be seen as open and friendly. However, people who fail to set and maintain boundaries with their families, ministries and careers often find that they have enough to do to meet their own needs, without others projecting their needs on them.

Everyone needs boundaries, not only to keep us out of trouble, but to keep trouble from invading our space. We must learn to set boundaries for ourselves, deciding what we will allow and what we will not. Then we must set boundaries for our coworkers, church members and neighbors. And yes, we must also set limits with family members and friends.

Boundaries are limits we set regarding how we allow others to treat us or to behave around us. We teach people how to treat us based on how strong or weak our boundaries are. Boundary setting is not about getting other people to change. It's about us deciding what we will and will not tolerate in our lives, and then communicating this firmly and consistently. Boundaries are the borders and limits that help us distinguish ourselves as separate from others.

As Christians, we should have spiritual boundaries. Spiritual boundaries are deliberate positions of faith. Spiritual boundaries tell the world what we will or will not tolerate in the body of Christ.

The Lord Himself gave us important guidance regarding the use of holy and healthy spiritual boundaries: "Let your 'Yes' mean 'Yes' and your 'No' mean 'No.' Anything more comes from the evil one" (Matthew 5:37). In that statement Jesus is saying that our boundaries must be clear.

For example, the world needs to know what we believe regardless to what is happening in the land. The nation is in a recession, and we are affected by it, but we do not live by it. The Bible declares: "The just shall live by faith"

(Romans 1:17). Therefore, Christians should be living recession-proof lives because God's economy is not impacted by the value of a dollar or the price of a barrel of oil. God is our source and He provides the resources that we need no matter what the world's economy looks like. "But my God shall supply all your need according to his riches in glory by Christ Jesus" (Philippians 4:19).

Spiritual boundaries have two sides to them. The first consists of everything you want inside that boundary such as the fruits of the spirit, love, holiness, sanctification, righteousness, prayer, etc. The second side consists of things that try to intrude beyond the line including: sin, hatred, stress, jealousy, depression, loneliness, and ungodly relationships.

I personally set pretty strict personal boundaries as it relates to work, church and when I will spend time with my sons. There are few exceptions to the boundaries I set in this regard.

I also set spiritual boundaries and I encourage you to do the same. Placing spiritual boundaries around you will protect you and keep you spiritually fit for the kingdom of God.

When we are clear about our boundaries, we know what behaviors we will accept or not accept from others (and ourselves), as well as what is appropriate for us and what is not.

I want to encourage you to take some time and check your fences, examine your boundaries and put up some new barbed wire when necessary.

Scripture Reading:

Titus 2:15
Speak these things, exhort, and rebuke with all authority. Let no one despise you.

Part Fifteen: Gifted To Be a Gift

Spiritual gifts are for strengthening others. This, of course, does not mean that the person who has a spiritual gift gets no joy or benefit from it, but it does suggest that gifts are given to be given.

To strengthen someone by a spiritual gift means to help their faith not give way as easily when trouble enters their life.

A spiritual gift is an expression of faith which aims to strengthen faith. It is activated from faith in us and aims for faith in another. Another way to put it would be this: A spiritual gift is an ability given by the Holy Spirit to express our faith effectively (in word or deed) for the strengthening of someone else's faith.

1 Peter 4:10-11, one of my favorite texts reminds us that "each has received a gift." Gifts are not for a few, but for all. God has gifted His children with talents, with time, with gifts, with graces, with finances and energy.

How have you invested what God has entrusted you with? I pray that you are using your gift to help others.

Does God Want You To Fulfill Vision Or Purpose?

Getting a vision does more to fuel passion than anything else I know. It will cause you to become highly motivated and self-disciplined. Proverbs 29:18 says, "Where there is no vision, the people perish." The New King James Version says, "Where there is no revelation, the people cast off restraint." The bottom line is that vision produces restraint or self-discipline, and the lack of it produces slackness.

The call to give birth to a vision means daring to be different. It means reordering your priorities according to your God-given destiny. If you think fulfilling a vision is easy, check the price tag! Like childbirth, it's hard, it's lonely, it's sleepless, it's appetite-changing, it's schedule-altering. It involves pain and even leaves stretch marks. So before you give lip service to a vision or play around with God's purpose for your life, ask yourself, "Am I ready to carry this vision full term?"

Visions are not for the immature, the impatient or the faint of heart. And you can't downsize them when things get tough. Esther's vision meant putting her life on the line and saying, "If I perish, I perish" (Esther 4:16). Did she perish? No, but she had to be willing to risk it. Are you?

Personally, I believe that man should have vision. Many of the pillars of the Bible (Abraham, Moses, etc.) were men of vision. Without vision the people perish, but I want us to look at this concept in a new light. I don't believe God operates out of vision but rather out of purpose. While vision is hopeful purpose is as good as done. In other words, His purposes will be accomplished no matter what else happens.

God does not merely *hope* that His plans will be fulfilled; He has made their accomplishment His priority.

Now, God does impart vision to us (Habakkuk. 2:2), but it is always in conformity with His purpose. In other words, a true vision from God is certain to be fulfilled, for it is the purpose of God revealed in advance.

I believe God gives everyone ideas and dreams because Proverbs 29:18 says, without a vision, we perish. But why are some Christians not pursuing their dreams? My theory is that they may have had their dreams crushed too many times, so that now they are fearful of dreaming again. Does this describe you? Maybe you're afraid to go after your dream just in case "it doesn't work out." But what if it did work out? You might as well release your faith and believe! Jesus said, "All things are possible to him who believes" (Mark 9:23).

I'm writing to encourage you to dream again. Does your vision have to be huge to be worthy? Absolutely not! However, I believe that your vision and mission should be God-given. If your vision/dream is God-given it will come to pass. Remember, a true vision from God is certain to be fulfilled, for it is the purpose of God revealed in advance.

There is a God-given dream inside you. Paul writes in Ephesians 2:10: "For we are God's masterpiece. He has created us anew in Christ Jesus, so that we can do the good things he planned (purposed) for us long ago."

Scripture Reading:

Hebrews 11:11
By faith even Sarah received ability to conceive even beyond the proper time of life, since she considered Him faithful who had promised.

What Could God Do Through You?

Has God ever given you a word? Has He given you a promise that He would do something great through you? How long has it been since you heard that word? Has that dream faded into a distant memory? Have you given up on His promise?

Abraham was seventy-five years old when God told him He would make him the father of many nations. And, as many of us do, Abraham began to lose hope when the promise took too long to materialize, and, in time he took things into his own hands, and had a son by his wife's maid.

Did that negate God's original promise? Not at all. Abraham was ninety-nine when he once again heard God's voice, reiterating the earlier promise to make him a great nation. And within one year that promised child was born. Stories like his abound in Scripture, so that we can be confident in the power of God. He's not limited the way we are. The truth is, He searches the earth for those who will dare to dream His dream, see His vision, and go for the gold, knowing that through God all things are possible.

So what could God do through you? Do you have a promise given long ago that you tucked in your heart waiting for its fulfillment? Well, I encourage you to take God at His word and wait on Him to bring it forth. Pray it in, believing God, and praise Him before you see any evidence of its arrival.

1 Corinthians 2:9 says: "Eye hath not seen nor ear heard, neither have entered into the heart of man the things which God hath prepared for them who love Him." What would happen if you made yourself available to God without reservation, willing to do something great?

I believe time is short, and He needs every one of us to be involved in changing the world, so if you make yourself available, be prepared for the extraordinary, because God isn't limited by our finite minds and limited talents. He can turn the simple things into the remarkable. In fact, 1 Corinthians 1:27 says, "But God hath chosen the foolish things of the world to confound the wise; and God hath chosen the weak things of the world to confound the things which are mighty…"

Nothing is too hard for God. Miracles, the improbable, the impossible… nothing is too hard for God. So, let me ask again, "What could God do through you?"

Scripture Reading

Hebrews 13:20-21
May the God of peace… equip you with everything good for doing his will, and may he work in us what is pleasing to him, through Jesus Christ, to whom be glory for ever and ever. (NIV)

Thinking Outside the Box

Do you ever find yourself limiting God? We as believers often limit God, assuming He'll do the same thing tomorrow that He did today. While that is sometimes true, He often wants to shake things up and do things another way. Does it upset you to face the unexpected, or do you like surprises?

Some of us value safety and security above all else, so that we essentially settle for them when God would prefer to do something grand and exciting. Perhaps God wants to develop a talent in you that you haven't yet discovered. Perhaps He wants to use you in a way that's outside your comfort zone. How would you feel about that?

Remember when you were small and everything was a huge adventure? Even a short walk in the woods brought wonder with every new step. What about now? Do you look at each day as a new adventure, or do you struggle to get out of bed to face the daily grind?

Part of the problem comes because we have lost our first love and no longer see God as the creative genius He is. We no longer see Him as the Master Designer with a great sense of humor who loves excitement. We no longer trust Him to keep us when things are unpredictable.

So how do we deal with that? We ask God to give us a fresh touch of heaven so we can see Him with new eyes, ready to change our routine into an odyssey.

Nothing is too hard for God. Rather, the problem is that we resist change and want to play it safe. What would happen if you let go of safety and security? I dare you to be bold and ask God to give you a fresh start. Ask Him to help you take risks as He opens doors, and see what He will do. You'll never know what you might have missed until you put aside your fears and step out in faith.

Scripture Reading:

1 Corinthians 2:19
Eye hath not seen nor ear heard, neither have entered into the heart of man the things that God has prepared for those who love Him.

Your Gift Makes Room For You

Wisdom comes in many forms. In the Bible, it is presented in the form of down-to-earth practical proverbs and the refined theological reflections of the Apostle Paul. It comes to us in the form of thundering prophetic words of rebuke and in the penetrating parables and stories told by Jesus Christ (as well as many other forms).

There is a world of difference between knowledge and wisdom. A knowledgeable person is simply a person who has a great deal of information and an abundance of ideas in his head. But having knowledge is not at all the same as being a wise person. Don't we all know really intelligent people who seem to be almost totally lacking in common sense or wisdom? While wisdom involves knowledge, it goes far beyond knowledge. Something else must be added to knowledge for it to transform into what we call wisdom.

There are many reasons why we need wisdom. For one, we need wisdom so we might live well. To live well is to know what the good life is and to orient one's self to live that way and seek that way of living. We need wisdom to make decisions that will enable us to move toward that goal. If one consistently lives for that vision and make choices that bring such a vision closer and closer, then they are living the good life. Wisdom is also needed so we may be of maximum assistance and service to others we meet.

How does one become wise? It would take an excessively long article to answer this question entirely, so I'll limit my reply to one answer. You must ask for wisdom from God. He is the source of all truth and wisdom (Colossians 2:2, 3). This is called prayer. Do what Solomon did, and pray for wisdom (James 1:5).

If ever anyone was qualified to speak of things pertaining to wisdom or knowledge, I would have to say that King Solomon would be a likely candidate. For the Scriptures tell us that God appeared unto Solomon in a dream and gave him this promise: "Lo, I have given thee a wise and an understanding heart; so that there was none like thee before thee, neither after thee shall any arise like unto thee" (I Kings 3:12).

The wisdom that God bestowed upon Solomon had nothing to do with human intellect or education, though unquestionably he possessed a high degree of these things also. The wisdom that he received from heaven however, was a wisdom that could not be learned in earthly institutions. Actually it is the capacity to see things as God sees them. Solomon was given the ability to see things as they really are--not according to man's opinion, but according to divine truth. This was the wisdom he needed, in order to execute righteous judgment among God's people of Israel, over whom God had appointed him king.

Solomon's wisdom surpassed the wisdom of all the people of the East, and all the wisdom of Egypt. He was wiser than anyone else...his fame spread throughout all the surrounding nations. He composed 3,000 proverbs, and songs numbering a 1,005. People came from all over the then-known world to hear the wisdom of Solomon; they came from all the kingdoms of the earth who had heard of his wisdom. (I Kings 4:29-34.)

When God appeared to Solomon with the promise of wisdom, He included something more to go along with it: "and I will give thee riches, and wealth, and honor, such as none of the kings have had that have been before thee, neither shall there any after thee have the like" (II Chronicles. 1:12). Solomon's set income alone was more than thirty tons of gold per year, "beside that which he had of the merchantmen, and of the traffic of the spice merchants, and of all the kings of Arabia, and of the governors of the country" (I Kings 10:14-15).

Solomon had a navy, which every three years came from foreign lands, "bringing [him] gold, and silver, ivory, and apes, and peacocks" (I Kings 10:22). All of his drinking vessels were of gold, for silver we are told, "was not anything accounted of in the days of Solomon" (II Chronicles 9:20). In fact, the Scripture says that silver was of no more worth to Solomon than stones (II Chronicles 9:27). His throne of ivory overlaid with pure gold was the most elaborate throne of any king in the world (II Chronicles. 9:17-19). In short, he was quite possibly the wealthiest man in the history of the world.

Concerning his authority and dominion, the Bible tells us: "And Solomon reigned over all kingdoms from the [Euphrates] river unto the land of the Philistines, and unto the border of Egypt: They brought presents **(gifts)**, and served Solomon all the days of his life" (I Kings 4:21). That is to say that he had rule over a significant portion of the existing world at that time.

The scripture says that "his fame was in all nations round about" (I Kings 4:31). "All the kings of the earth sought the presence of Solomon, to hear the wisdom that God had put in his heart. And they brought every man his present **(gift),** vessels of silver, and vessels of gold, and raiment, harness, and spices, horses and mules, a rate year by year" (II Chronicles 9:23,24).

Time and space will not allow us to continue to describe the full magnitude of the majestic grandeur of Solomon's unparalleled life, but I must add that in the days of Solomon, the search for wisdom led to the palace of a legendary, wise and prosperous king.

The Book of Proverbs displays the wisdom of King Solomon. Under the direct inspiration of God, he shares with you His experiences as king. In Proverbs 18:16 he writes:

"A man's gift maketh room for him,
and bringeth him before great men."

The Proverb speaks of a man's **gift** making room for him--opening doors of opportunity and privilege that were otherwise out of reach. Do you recognize your gift?

Your Gift

Every child of God is born with gifts and talents inside, kicking and screaming for expression. This is not something we learn but something God has given us. It is the part of you that defines and describes who you are. Nobody can exercise this gift in quite the same way you can. You were made for this gift and the gift was made for you.

Gifts are varied. We are not born with equal gifts. We are given different spiritual gifts for service. Paul emphasized the universality of gifts. "*Unto everyone of us* is given grace according to the measure of the gift of Christ" (Ephesians 4:7 italics added). More than once Paul used analogy of the human body with its many members--eyes, ears, hands, and feet--to illustrate varied gifts in the body of Christ. "Ye are the body of Christ and members in particular" (1 Corinthians 12:27).

Your gift cannot be divorced from your character. Your character matches the gift inside you. For example, if you are a person who is lazy and irresponsible before you received a spiritual gift, you may be just as lazy and irresponsible after receiving your gift. You may preach like an angel, but arrive late for every speaking engagement.

God has bestowed an incredible gift in the heart of every believer. You do not have to invent your gift, but you must open it. Please allow someone to help you open your heart to uncover your gift for the glory of God.

A Man's Gift….. Maketh Room For Him

One of the least understood principles of success, but one of the most vital is this--your God-given gift will make room for you! Proverbs 18:16 is a powerful statement where Solomon reveals that gifts serve a noble purpose in obtaining favor and rewarding kindness. (I Kings 5:1-12; 10:1-13.)

The phrase *A man's gift maketh room for him* shows the power of gifts, that is, a good present (gift) will go far.

A man's gift maketh room for him indicates that when you develop the potential that is within you and God gives you a gift through His Holy Spirit, then you will become successful.

A man's gift maketh room for him means it "enlarges him," brings him out of prison, or out difficulties that have pressed down on him. It makes way for him to go before a judge, and for a favorable hearing of his case.

A man's gift maketh room for him enlarges his acquaintances, and brings him respect among men. It opens a way for him into the presence and company of great men, in honor and power. It renders him acceptable, and appeases anger; as in the cases of Jacob and Abigail. (Genesis 32:20, 43:11, 1 Samuel 25:27.)

God has put a gift in every person that the world will make room for. For every gift God bestows, the Spirit has planned a sphere of service. You are given an outlet for your gift to minister to others.

If your *gift makes room for you*, how do you package or present your gift for distribution? Does your gift express how much someone means to you or how much you care about them? Does your gift indicate that the receiver is someone special? Is your gift meaningful? Does it reflect love, care and affection? Is your gift wrapped in deep emotions? Does your gift reflect the relationship between you and the recipient? Does your gift reflect the relationship between you and God? Is your gift of good quality? Is your gift in demand and desirable? Does it reflect generosity?

Or is your gift packaged with pride, anger, jealousy, a lack of compassion, laziness? Do others look at your gift and say your value is declining or it's not a good offering? Do people refuse your gift because it's not useable, because it's outdated or has been misused?

God is the Giver of every good gift (James 1:7). This scripture implies that all gifts that truly bless us are God's gifts. Therefore, when you give a good gift to someone, it should bless their life and glorify God.

A Man's Gift...Brings Him Before Great Men

The second part of Proverbs 18:16 says, "A man's gift...brings him before great men". It gains entrance to the presence of those superior to the giver.

In Bible days, a gift was used for access to a prophet. You didn't approach a royal person in the Bible without bringing a gift. In order to meet a king, you brought him a gift. When you went to see a prophet, you brought him a gift because a gift shows honor and respect. Your gift gave you access to great men, and through the gift you were presented to great men.

- David's instrument (gift) brought him before King Saul (1 Sam 16:23).
- The three wise men brought gifts in order to meet baby Jesus (Math 2:11).
- Jacob used a gift to appease Esau (Gen. 32:3-21). He also sent gifts for favor in Pharaoh's court (Gen 43:11-14). Joseph's gift brought him before Pharaoh.
- Abraham's servant found a bride for Isaac with gifts (Gen. 24:53).

- Ehud used a gift for his errand (Judges 3:15-23).
- Abigail cooled David's heart with a needed gift for his men (I Sam. 25:18,35

Many people came to Solomon and brought him gifts because of his wisdom. They were so in awe of his God-given intellect that they wanted to show him how appreciative they were to be in his presence.

Your gift suggests what you think of the person you going to meet. You don't approach royalty and not give them something of quality. This is why we give offerings/tithes (gifts) to God. Your gift to God implies what you think of Him. 2 Corinthians 8:12 says "If the willingness is there, the gift is acceptable according to what one has, not according to what he does not have." Deuteronomy 16:16-17 declares, "No man should appear before the LORD empty-handed: Each of you must bring a gift in proportion to the way the LORD your God has blessed you."

We are blessed when we give. God wants us to give because he knows how blessed we will be as we give generously to him and to others.

Gift exchanges are not the lesson here, but rather a private and personal gift from one person to another. When you greet great people, you bring a gift, expecting nothing in return.

My friend, the gift you're sitting on is valuable, priceless. When you exercise it God's way, not only will the world make room for you, but it will also pay you for it.

It is your gift that is the key to your success. Why not make room for yourself in the world by using your gift?

Scripture Reading:

Proverbs 18:16
*A **gift** opens the way for the giver and ushers him into the presence of the great. (NIV)*

Deuteronomy 16:17
*Each of you must bring a **gift** in proportion to the way the LORD your God has blessed you. (NIV)*

1 Kings 10:25
*Year after year, everyone who came brought a **gift** --articles of silver and gold, robes, weapons and spices, and horses and mules. (NIV)*

2 Kings 8:8
*he said to Hazael, "Take a **gift** with you and go to meet the man of God. (NIV)*

2 Corinthians 8:12
*For if the willingness is there, the **gift** is acceptable according to what one has, not according to what he does not have. (NIV)*

God Can Arise Through the Pain of Your Suffering

If you have been encouraged and challenged by Barbara Bryant in **Gifted Inspirations**, here is another book, written in the same encouraging style, that we think you will enjoy:

Suffering has the potential to leave individuals wounded if they attempt to maneuver, in their own strength, through life's challenges. Seldom do women and men alike, read books that carefully guide them from the realities and horrors of suffering to a more joyous perspective of suffering.

Compensated Suffering is inspiring for both men and women who have ever questioned the purpose of multiple and diverse trials! From chapter to chapter, encouragement leaps into your spirit as Barbara Bryant walks you through her personal and spiritual journey to a new paradigm of suffering—a paradigm built upon faith, forgiveness and renewal. Whether your suffering has manifested itself as a physical ailment, abuse, financial hardship or even a lengthy "holding" period, Barbara eloquently shares the new possibilities in God that can arise through the pain of suffering!